"BEING ME is a wise and comprehensive guide that integrates the theory and the experience of our psychological development and path of healing. Using the analogy of building a house it outlines each stage of emotional and interpersonal development, and the tasks for healing ourselves when our attachment experiences have been less than optimal. Written in a warm and accessible way this book contains inspiration, education and practical advice for healing and personal development. This book is rich in scope and depth and will repay multiple readings providing hope and guidance for the long but worthwhile journey of recovery from emotional wounds and reaching your full potential."

Ally Lawrence, MPsych - *Clinical Psychologist,* Australia

"BEING ME is a beautiful book that will be useful to me for a long time. In the past, when I read books of a similar vein (psychology/self-help), I found myself feeling ashamed, guilty or less than in my plight to better myself. Not in this case! BEING ME has been written with such heartfelt compassion, that even though some of the content had me delving into the shadow parts of myself, the author Maree B. Even guided me through it so lovingly that I felt *held* throughout the process. The way Maree explains concepts is very clear and the exercises that support the explanations are practical and easy to do. I related to this book so much and felt, at times, that it was written for me. Maree's approach to explaining and guiding the reader is truly a *whole being* approach. The beginning of the book dedicates itself to ALL of you, and this deeper meaning is not lost on me. Thank you for such an important book and message."

Melissa Georgiou, MEd - author of *Mindfulness Made Easy*

"BEING ME is a great read, incorporating scientific evidence and personal experience in a way that is both engaging and educational. I particularly enjoyed the section on emotional balance and regulation. The exercises which are included within each chapter provide a wonderful experiential component."

Rachael Williams, MPsych - *Clinical Psychologist,* Australia

Being Me

Being Me

Healing your Attachment Wounds and Becoming Whole

Maree B. Even

MBE Psychology Publishing

This book is intended for educational purposes only. It is not a replacement for individual psychological assessment, treatment or advice. Please seek the services of a registered psychologist if you require assistance.

Cover Design by Maree B. Even
Cover Image: Shutterstock

NATIONAL LIBRARY OF AUSTRALIA

A catalogue record for this book is available from the National Library of Australia

ISBN-978-0-6485753-0-6

For ALL of you

About the Author

Maree B. Even is a Clinical Psychologist in Perth, Western Australia. She works in private practice providing psychotherapy and supervision. See www.mbepsychology.com.au

Contents

Preface

After many years of assisting others in their therapeutic journey, my own unfinished psychological business started to call me with greater insistence. Over the years I had done sessions with a few different therapists, but this time I knew I was ready for something deeper. I rang a psychodynamic psychotherapist my friend had recommended, and thus began my five-and-a-half-year therapeutic journey. It was midway during this process that I started to write this book.

I began to wonder about the path of therapy, healing or repair. I was an insider on the journey and wanted to understand the process I was undertaking. And being a psychotherapist myself, I wanted to have greater clarity about what would benefit the people that came to see me.

I also think this question, about the path of therapy, was sparked as a result of my experience as a meditation practitioner. I had been practicing meditation in the Buddhist tradition for many years. Here there is a path, or numerous paths depending on which school of Buddhism you follow, to becoming more "Awake". These paths have been handed down from teacher to student for thousands of years; they are well trodden and mapped out for the dedicated practitioner. Although the path of becoming more spiritually awake is not mutually exclusive to the path of healing our psychological wounds, there are important differences.

I became curious. Are there similar paths for psychological growth and becoming more whole as a person? And more specifically, are there paths for healing our attachment wounds which affect our sense of self and the way we function in relationships and the world? This curiosity was the spark to begin writing this book.

It has taken me three years to craft this written work. Just as my journey of *becoming* fully human will continue throughout my life, I hope what I have written is not seen as definitive, but something which remains alive and grows with each person who reads it.

Interestingly, upon completion of this book, the following question arose in my mind: If I needed to trek through the Amazon Jungle, who would I want as my guide? Someone indigenous to this forest, or a Harvard Professor who had spent their lifetime studying it. It's taken me a little while to contemplate this question, but I think I have my answer for now. If it was someone indigenous, I would want them to have knowledge of how to guide someone who is unfamiliar with this forest. If it was the Harvard Professor, I would want them to have personally undertaken the trek.

I tell this story, as throughout writing this book I utilised both subjective (i.e. the indigenous person) and objective (i.e. the Harvard Professor) points of view. Subjectively, I remembered and noticed my own experience of healing and growth, as well as that of others I've had the privilege to guide on their journey. Objectively, I researched and read what others in the psychological sciences and neurosciences had found and thought. Including both viewpoints, I think, has contributed to a richer and more whole perspective which could not have been achieved with either one on its own.

I have written this book as a journey we are taking together as fellow human beings. There are three parts.

Part I is the beginning. It includes the underlying concepts, theories and framework for this journey of healing your attachment wounds and becoming whole.

Part II is the main road. I have divided this section into four phases of psychological development. In each phase, I describe what a child needs from their early attachment relationships to grow into a secure and whole person. I then discuss what can occur, to your sense of self and your experience of relationship, if you didn't get some of these needs met in a "good enough" way. Most importantly, I illuminate a path of repair, so you may heal your wounds of attachment and become a person who feels more secure, connected, real and whole.

Part III is the final section of this expedition. It describes three guidelines; emotion, relationship and time. I have used these as the major guiding principles which underlie this psychological work. Knowing and heeding these will assist you on this therapeutic journey.

The path to healing and becoming whole is a step by step exploration and discovery, with many twists and turns. Since at times it can feel like you are navigating your way in the dark, it is my sincere hope that this book shed some light on your journey.

THE JOURNEY OF HEALING AND BECOMING WHOLE CAN

BE CHALLENGING. WE CONFRONT OUR DARKEST DEMONS,

LEAP ACROSS CHASMS WE THOUGHT WE COULD NOT

CROSS AND COME HOME TO PLACES INSIDE OURSELVES WE

NEVER KNEW WERE THERE. IT TAKES COURAGE TO STEP

ONTO THIS PATH, AND EVERY SINGLE BIT OF OUR

STRENGTH TO KEEP GOING.

~ ♥ ~

PART I

PART I

Introduction

Our childhood is supposed to be a time of safety, protection, nurturing, exploration and growth. It is a time when we are fully dependent on those that brought us into the world, to provide this for us. This care giving, usually happens in a way which is "good enough". This is a term coined by Donald Winnicott, describing a parent who is devoted enough to take care of their baby and child, in a way which is attuned to their needs at each stage of development. [a]

Statistically the majority of children have received this "good enough" parenting; at least 50% and possibly as much as 70%. In the remaining cases however, something goes awry, and the child does not get what they need to develop and grow into a psychologically healthy and mature individual. These are the children this book is primarily dedicated to. We are adults now, but still we may hold this legacy in our hearts; unless further along in our development as grown children, adolescents or adults, we experienced at least one relationship where we felt safe, supported, cared about and free to express our authentic self. Again, the benefits here occur when the relationship has been "good enough".

---

[a] Donald Winnicott was particularly concerned with mothers as it was the 1960's, when mothers were usually the primary caregivers. Today however, although mothers are often this in the beginning, the father (or other support person) may also take on this role early on. I will therefore say parent or caregiver.

Interestingly, relationships in childhood do not need to perfectly meet all our requirements for us to grow in a psychologically healthy way. In fact, not only is this impossible, but also undesirable. Age-appropriate challenge and frustrations allows us the opportunity to build resilience, reduce illusions about reality and grow to engage in reciprocal relationships.

A bit like an elastic band being stretched, failures in relationship are okay, to a certain degree, as a child can assimilate the resultant frustration and disappointment. This frustration and disappointment must be developmentally appropriate, titrated and experienced as tolerable, to then result in the positive outcomes suggested. When the failures in relationship are outside the child's developmental capability, too big or too continuous, the positive outcomes will not be realised. A little like an elastic band stretched too far will eventually break, a child cannot learn from frustrations and disappointments which result in intolerable emotional arousal.[1]

A core aspect of life is relationship, in every form. The way we engage and disengage in these relationships is heavily determined by both our innate tendencies (such as temperament) and our lived experience in relationship. Our earliest connections (i.e. with our caregivers) have a profound impact.[2] This is when we implicitly learn what it means to be a human in connection (or disconnection) with another.

If our relationships early in life are "good enough", we grow with a sense of security and trust, knowing we, others and the world are generally okay. Our relationships become a means of connection, belonging, warmth, support, enjoyment, growth and reciprocity of needs being met.

However, if early in life our relationships are not "good

enough", our experience of self, others and the world will be quite different. We may grow experiencing our self and relationships as unimportant, all-consuming or a source of pain. Relationships become something we defend against, feel preoccupied with, or protect ourselves from, and so we generally find it difficult to feel secure and satisfied. Considering the very essence of life and being human is about connection, feelings of insecurity and dissatisfaction within our self and our relationships is an enormous loss, and profoundly affects our time on earth.

There will be many among us who resonate with this sense of insecurity, and yearn for fulfilment within our self, our relationships and our life. If we relate to these feelings, we may need to devote energy and purpose into examining and repairing this insecurity and lack of wholeness. However, in saying this, all of us to some extent have parts of our self that require this examination and repair. Some of us will have it to a greater extent, while others will have it to a lesser extent. Even though the degree of work that needs to be done will differ amongst us, we are ALL called to do this work; sharing this journey of discovering our full human beingness.

In writing, I hold a candle of hope so we may ALL reclaim our wholeness. In this journey, we are called to heal our wounds of disconnection and claim back forgotten parts of ourselves. Then as we walk this earth in connection with all that is inside us and all that is outside us, we come to know what it truly means to be alive.

"THE GREATEST HAZARD OF ALL, LOSING ONE'S SELF, CAN OCCUR VERY QUIETLY IN THE WORLD, AS IF IT WERE NOTHING AT ALL. NO OTHER LOSS CAN OCCUR SO QUIETLY; ANY OTHER LOSS – AN ARM, A LEG, FIVE DOLLARS, A WIFE, ETC, - IS SURE TO BE NOTICED."
Soren Kierkegaard In The Sickness Unto Death. Kierkegaard's Writings Vol19

A Touch of Theory

Our experience in utero, through to our second year, profoundly impacts our development.[3] As newborns coming into this world we are extremely vulnerable, particularly in the first nine months of life and then until about two to three years of age.

In comparison to every other species, we remain helpless and fully dependent the longest outside our mother's womb. Our newborn brain is much less developed compared to other newborn mammals. For example, if a human brain upon birth, is to be comparable to that of a newborn chimpanzee, it is estimated we would need to have an eighteen to twenty-one-month gestation, rather than the usual nine.[4]

The first nine months outside the womb is sometimes referred to as the external gestation period, exemplifying the importance of this time for a newborn's growth and development.[5] Our brain, at that time, is about a quarter of the size of what we now have as an adult. Once born, our brain and nervous system continue to develop rapidly in the first few years of life.[6] At two years of age it is at 80% capacity, and by three years almost fully developed at 90%.[7]

During these first three years of growth, we need a responsive caregiver to assist regulate our physiological, neuro-biological and psychological functioning and development.[8] In the initial several months, our caregiver's physical touch and devoted relationship is how this occurs.[9] As we begin to crawl, walk and gain a sense of self, the ongoing attachment relationship, with a caregiver attuned to our evolving needs of separation and individuation, is the most critical factor for our development.

To summarise, relationship is the most potent ingredient in our development. In the science world this is now irrefutably agreed upon.[10]

"EARLY INTERPERSONAL RELATIONSHIPS, FOR BETTER OR WORSE, PROFOUNDLY AND INDELIBLY IMPACT THE PSYCHOLOGICAL, PHYSIOLOGICAL, AND NEUROBIOLOGICAL ASPECTS OF THE EARLY DEVELOPMENT OF THE SELF."
Allan N. Shore (2012). In, The Science of the Art of Psychotherapy, p:227

Attachment Theory and Separation-Individuation Theory are used in this book as underlying psychological frameworks to assist understanding. It is not to "type" us. We are complex creatures, with both habitual character aspects and a fluid nature. No theory can describe us completely or reflect our (and others) actual subjective experience. At best, they are useful signposts allowing us to comprehend complex phenomena. Both these theories provide an acute awareness of relationship as fundamental to psychological growth and development.[11]

For those who want to know more about the original aspects of these theories, I have provided a description of each in the Appendix section of this book. Below, I describe the different attachment styles (secure, insecure-avoidant, insecure-ambivalent and disorganised/disorientated) and how they may impact our self and relational style in adulthood.

It is postulated that our sense of self and how we relate with others, as adults, have their beginnings in the attachment relationships we had as children. If then, we had a **secure attachment** as a child, we probably had caregivers who were generally attuned to our needs in a "good enough" way. We learnt we can get our needs met and are free to explore our world with confidence, as our caregivers were available when we needed them. As a result, we generally feel successful in the world, know we can influence others and master the tasks we need to.[12] Since we learnt reciprocity from our caregivers, we also engage in mutually satisfying relationships. Through our caregivers meeting our needs, we can now as an adult, meet our own needs and be empathic and respond when others show their needs. We are generally socially competent, have successful relationships, can regulate our own emotions and feel worthy, lovable, cooperative and capable.[13] This secure attachment enables us to cope with an ever-expanding range of relationships and experiences over our lifetime, as well as maintain long-term connections with others.

If however, we had an **insecure attachment** of either *avoidance*[b] or *ambivalence*,[c] we probably had caregivers who were either rejecting of our needs (including emotional and physical contact) and/or inconsistent in their parenting responses. As a result of this "not good enough" parenting, we learnt we cannot get our needs consistently met in relationship and so developed strategies to defend against this reality.

We may now have difficulty meeting our own needs and being responsive to the needs of others, therefore compromising our ability to engage in reciprocal and satisfying relationships. If we have more of an *avoidant* attachment, we may tend towards aggression, toughness and hard-heartedness, perhaps as a defence against

---

[b] An insecure-avoidant attachment style in adulthood is sometimes referred to as "dismissing" or just "avoidant"..

[c] An insecure-ambivalent attachment style in adulthood is sometimes referred to as "pre-occupied", "anxious-ambivalent" or just "anxious".

rejection.[14] In relationship, we may minimise our need for the other, blame them when conflict arises and feel less supported. If we have a more *ambivalent* attachment, we tend to be more anxious and dependent in our relationships, vigilant about getting our needs met and focus on the other to the exclusion of our own autonomy.[15]

With an insecure attachment, we are also less adept at regulating our own emotions and tend to use external means to assist with this regulation. If we are more *avoidant*, we tend to dismiss and minimise emotion. We probably use non-relational forms such as alcohol, drugs, medication, food, books, work, ambition, achievement, power or sexual conquests to help soothe and regulate our inner world. If we are more *ambivalent*, we may hold onto our emotions and maximise their expression. We are probably more introspective, believe we are flawed and tend to cling to our partner and other relationships to regulate our inner world and feel better.[16]

We may also find it difficult to hold in mind a balance of both the good (e.g. strengths, feelings of love) and bad (e.g. limitations, feelings of hate) of our self and others. If we have an *avoidant* attachment, we may be more aware of our strengths and find it difficult to acknowledge our limitations. Conversely, when it comes to others, we may be overly focused on their limitations and the negative feelings we have towards them. If we have an *ambivalent* attachment, we may be more aware of our limitations, while not acknowledging our strengths. With others however, we may overly focus on their strengths and our positive feelings about them. It is also possible we engage in both dynamics, depending upon the relational situation. So sometimes we may be more like the avoidant style, while at other times we are more like the ambivalent style. The underlying factor, in both these dynamics, is that we find it difficult to tolerate the conflictual feelings we have about our self and others. This means, we probably feel less stable and whole in our sense of self, as well as have trouble maintaining long-term reciprocal relationships.

If we had a **disorganised/disorientated attachment**,[d] our caregivers were probably frightening (e.g. abusive and/or grossly neglectful) or frightened themselves (e.g. unresolved trauma or loss, or gross lack of support in parenting). The parenting we received was "not good enough" and could have been harmful or traumatic. In this case, we were not free to learn, explore and grow, as our attention was focused on how to survive. Since our caregivers were frightening or frightened, we developed strategies to reduce our terror, including withdrawal, dissociation, distraction, avoidance, submission and/or aggression. As adults, we tend to keep away from intimacy as we learnt relationships are confusing, frightening and dangerous.[17] Since we experienced harm, gross inconsistency and/or neglect from our caregivers, we do not trust others and are hyper-vigilant and fearful. Consequently, we tend to protect and fend for ourselves, not expecting others to meet our needs for care and support. We get what is needed in any way we can, passively accepting what others give us as we do not think we can affect our world. [18]

These categories of attachment are probably not as static or dichotomous as represented here. Such a delineated approach would not give a true nor rich enough portrayal of our human complexity and variety. For example, people who seem to have a secure attachment style may also have elements of avoidance, ambivalence and maybe even disorganisation or disorientation, given the right

---

[d] A disorganised/disorientated attachment style in adulthood is sometimes referred to as "fearful-avoidant".

circumstances. Perhaps with the insecure styles of avoidance and ambivalence, there is also not such a clear demarcation as suggested. Indeed, it is likely we have elements of all these styles, but differ in the degree to which we exhibit them, depending upon the relational situation we find ourselves in. Furthermore, it is possible that there are other intricacies in attachment styles that to date have not been recognised, so the categories presented here may not encompass the full breadth of relational styles.

We must also be cautious in stating attachment style in childhood predicts attachment style in adulthood. The research, using correlational data, shows our early learning about relationship influences the way we relate as adults. However, this data cannot show cause and effect. In addition, there are many further stages of development and potential mitigating factors that occur between childhood and adulthood, which can affect our individual style of relating. Interestingly, research conducted with the Adult Attachment Interview has found that to be scored as a secure-autonomous attachment style, in adulthood, the person needs to be able to reflect on and describe both the positives and negatives of the relationship with their parents, in a coherent and open manner.[19] This does not mean they necessarily had a secure attachment as a child. But possibly, were either lucky enough to have other positive attachment experiences in their lives or were able to *work through* the attachment wounding experienced as a child.

In this book then, I would like to allow room for both perspectives. That is, the tendency to inhabit our early attachment model of relationship, as well as the potential for fluidity, growth and change in this model.

A Building Metaphor

As an infant and child, our self is implicitly shaped by the relationship we have with our caregivers.[20] Our relational experiences at this time, form the bedrock of our development.

Symbolically, this is akin to building a house. For a house to be stable it requires a good foundation and an adequate structure. If a house is built on unstable land or has an unsound foundation, structural problems are inevitable. If however, the land and foundation is strong and sturdy, then what is built upon it, if also constructed satisfactorily, will remain resilient and be able to weather various storms, without splitting, cracking or crumbling.

If we take this metaphor further and see ourselves as this house, we might consider the type of land the foundation is initially laid on, as the first important factor in our development. Building foundations need to be laid on ground which is stable and secure. If there is any doubt about the land's stability much preparation is done to ensure its strength, allowing the foundation to then be laid with confidence. This part of our development may be seen as occurring from conception and more specifically, for the purposes of this book, from birth to about 3-6 months. If upon birth, the ground is not adequate, foundational development will go awry. If however, the land is stable enough to securely hold the foundational beginning of the newborn infant, we are off to a very good start.

Phase 1: Safe and sound ground (conception/birth to 3-6 months)

In the second phase, we lay the foundation of our house. This concerns our experience from approximately 3-6 months to 15 months. This is where the basis of our development is cemented. Again, if this is not tended to adequately, it may eventually form cracks and jeopardise the structure of the building (i.e. our self) that rests upon it. We would then need to organise our developing self around these foundational faults. This means we have a less resilient structure and a greater susceptibility to future problems.

Phase 2: A solid and secure foundation (3-6months to 15 months)

In the third phase, we build the structure of our house. This relates to the development of a separate self in relationship to others. This occurs primarily in our toddler years (15 months to 3 - 4 years). Here, our *whole* self needs to be seen, related to and encouraged to flourish; with a balance of being indulged and having limits set. Our relationships assist us in the struggle of balancing our grandiosity and vulnerability, power and powerlessness and needs of dependence and independence. If this doesn't occur, our self will feel unstable; requiring external means to prop us up.

Phase 3: A well-constructed house (15 months to 3-4years)

The fourth phase is the completion of our house into a home, to then be lived in amongst a community of other homes. This is related to our early childhood and preschool years of 3-4 to 6-7 years of age. Here, we begin to go out into the wider world (e.g. begin school) and thus experience a broadening of our relationships and sense of self. During this time, we need to feel worthy for who we are, rather than what we do. We also start to become more aware of our emerging psycho-sexuality, bringing themes of love, self-expression, sexuality and competition to the forefront. Finally, in this phase, we begin to experience our self and others as stable, complex and basically okay. This budding psychological maturity allows us to cope with an ever-expanding range of relationships and experiences over our lifetime.

Phase 4: A Home (3-4 years to 6-7 years)

From here, in our development, we have a *self* which we will generally inhabit throughout our lives. In the years to come, we might re-decorate and even renovate, adding another room, extending the kitchen, painting, etc. But we still have the original foundation and house initially built. In the same way, whilst all our later relationships and experiences have a significant impact on us, we tend to fit them into the construction of our self which has already been established.

There are however, at least two possible ways our self may significantly change after this point. The first being, if at some future time in our lives we experience something extremely traumatic. For example, if we have been in an accident, assaulted, raped, tortured or in a war zone. In these cases, if we felt our survival was under threat, the experience is so unbearable that our sense of self and place in the world is completely shaken. This is likened to a storm, flood or earthquake, which rocks the very structure or foundation of our house.

The second way, our self may change, is if we experience a relationship which is *healing*. For example, if we didn't have a "good enough" relational experience in our early years, later in life we might decide to engage in a therapeutic relationship. This allows us to internalise a new experience of relationship and sense of who we are, so over time we may become more secure and whole. We may also feel fundamentally changed through a relationship with an intimate partner, a friend, a spiritual teacher or even while parenting a child.

This building metaphor is perhaps a way to more easily understand how we, from birth through childhood, develop and grow. I acknowledge, each of us is an individual and infinitely more complex than a metaphor can reflect. However, perhaps it is a useful starting point and something we can refer to as we journey on.

Repair

Implied in this building metaphor is the idea that the earlier our house experienced construction problems, the more work there is to examine and repair. Generally, it is much easier to repair a house which has been built on solid land, has a good foundation and is structurally sound. Any builder would say, "Yeah no problem". If our house is not so structurally sound however, that same builder might slowly rub their chin and explain that some supporting beams are required to make it stronger. "It needs quite a bit of work, but certainly possible".

If however, the foundation or land our house was built upon is unstable, the builder might say, "Sorry no can do". Since we don't take the first "no" as conclusive, we decide to get a second opinion. This second builder, who we know has done something like this before, takes a thorough assessment of our land, foundation and house. We see the tension in their facial muscles as they place their hand heavily on their forehead. Our heart deflates as hope slowly disappears; the first builder was probably right after all. Just when we're about to tell this builder not to worry, they look us squarely in the eye.

"It's a big job."

We stay rooted to the ground; ears pricked, mouth shut tight.

They breathe...deeply. Again, they look at us, almost like they're checking if we can stand what needs to be done. "It'll take a long time."

We nod, perhaps a little over enthusiastically. Partly because we really have no idea what is involved, but mainly because our whole house will collapse if we don't do something.

"But," they start again, "If you're patient, allow time for the work to be done, have the courage to keep going when it gets tough and most of all trust this is possible, then it might be feasible."

We nod soberly. We prefer a sure thing, not the uncertainty they are alluding to. "Hard work, patience, courage and trust...okay!"

Some of us may wonder, (and I have often thought this too), if it is possible to go so far back and examine the initial assembly of our house or self. The answer I have come to, is yes, it is possible. The second question then arises, is it possible, after examining and identifying a shaky foundation, for example, to repair it? The answer to this again is yes, given we firstly have a realistic understanding of what repair means, and secondly, we have the elements which have been shown to contribute towards repair.

So let's become a little clearer about what *repair* actually means. The most descriptive way to do this I think is with an analogy. In this case it is the Japanese art form of "Kintsugi". Kintsugi means "golden joinery" and is a technique for repairing broken pottery with lacquer or resin, sprinkled with gold (silver or platinum) powder. The breakages and repairs are treated as part of the history of the object, rather than something which needs to be disguised. The objects which are repaired often become works of art, as it is believed the broken places which have been highlighted bring greater beauty to the piece than was possible without the break. This is what the Japanese call "Wabi-sabi"; an embracing of the flawed or imperfect.

When I think about repair and what it means, I think about the art of Kintsugi and the philosophy of Wabi-sabi. Our wounds are a part of our history and cannot be erased, but with the work of repair we may be strengthened and made whole. We may build a more robust and resilient self, to act as the container for the flow of our emotional world. This allows us the strength and capacity to be with our internal world and interact with the external world, without being worried about going to pieces, falling apart, breaking or being too fragile.

Although we cannot change who we fundamentally are, in repair, we may become whole and real. We will not be the same as someone who has not had our history. But we may be a person, who having faced adversity, stands strong; with the wisdom of seeing even our deepest scars as a creative part of who we (and others) are.

Further on in this book I have written more about the *process* of repair. Since every situation and person is unique, I am cautious about making generalisations. However, considering there are many ideas about the notion of repair (or healing and therapy), I wanted to begin by offering a realistic understanding of what this might mean. Keeping this in mind, we may now discuss the characteristics shown to generally contribute towards repair.

The first aspect which impacts the possibility of repair are the qualities of the person undertaking this work. Some of these include our willingness to do the work, whether our life is conducive to such work, if we have the means (e.g. time, finances) and the amount of effort we put in. We might wonder, what is meant by *work* and *effort*. Firstly, rather than being a passive recipient, we actively engage in the repair process. That is, we can creatively use what is available to us for healing and growth.[21] Secondly, we are, over time, able to contact and contain the emotional experiences we avoid.[22] Since this type of work takes time and can be extremely tough at some points, it can require us to draw on every ounce of our inner strength and "gentle warrior spirit".

The second factor which affects the possibility of repair, relates to the builder or person (e.g. registered therapist) we are doing this work with. It is important this person has experience and knowledge in this area, has done their own healing work and is able to walk beside us through the twists and turns down our rabbit hole. Their level of self-awareness and emotional maturity will determine their ability to assist us.[23] In essence, the other person may aid the development of our consciousness, only to the extent of their own conscious evolvement. Consequently, it is important to choose wisely the person we do this psychological work with. Have they done their own therapeutic work? Does what they say, feel as if it comes from a place of personal knowing, or does it feel as if they are repeating what someone else has told them?[24] Are they emotionally present?

Finally, the match or chemistry between these two people, accounts for much of the variability in outcome. This is where it becomes increasingly complex, as it is difficult to specifically define what these characteristics are. Perhaps, this is because what each needs and is looking for in the other is often somewhat unconscious, particularly in the beginning. It has been suggested that the two people probably need to have enough in common (re: attachment and relating styles, values and emotional make-up) to have an attuned and comfortable connection, but enough difference to aid growth and keep the relationship interesting and dynamic.[25] Since repair occurs through the vehicle of relationship, it is important we feel safe, listened to, and that the person we do this work with demonstrates some understanding of us. Then to enable growth and change, we also need to feel challenged to new ways of thinking and being.[26]

Some of us may wonder why we would do this repair work at all, especially since it sounds like hard work. We might think, "Can't I just leave my house as it is and be happy with it, even if there are some structural issues". The answer to this is a bit of a paradox.

Being happy with it is a sound idea. In fact, no matter how our current house (or self) seems, we can acknowledge we are "good enough" right now. We are not broken or wrong in any way and do not need to be fixed or made right.

Still, when our house has a leak in the roof, for example, we repair the leak; otherwise our house may flood or at best get damp and smelly. Or if our foundations are insecure, causing cracks in our walls, we probably need to repair it, so our house stands strong. In the same way a house needs to be maintained and rested on a stable foundation for it to be okay, so do we.

Moreover, if there is a structural issue with our house, strain is placed on other parts, thus compensating for the problem. This is the same with us. If we experience difficulty in a part of our psychological organisation, other parts of us are put under strain. Basically, we expend valuable energy holding ourselves together, so we don't fall apart. Because we've always had to do this, we might not be aware of the strain this puts us under. It's a bit like if we've lived our life standing on one leg, we wouldn't know how tiring and unsteady this is compared to having two feet firmly on the ground.

Development of Self

G iven our house (or self) is constructed when we're very young, we are usually not consciously aware of how it occurred. We might have some specific memories of our early childhood and an inkling of what it was generally like. But still, we would find it difficult to say the exact circumstances which brought about who we experience ourselves to be today. This process is referred to in psychology as the development of "self". It is mostly completed without our conscious awareness, as the brain mechanisms for understanding and making sense of our experiences are undeveloped, particularly in the very early phases.

First important point: Our "self" is mostly constructed unconsciously or implicitly.[27]

The bricks with which our house (or self) is constructed, are our experiences. Like a house is built brick by brick, our self is built experience by experience. Experience here relates to the constant interaction between our internal and external relational worlds. These relational experiences, even if we cannot remember them, are implicitly built into the walls of our evolving self.

Second important point: Our "self" becomes constructed through our relational experiences.[28]

These relational experiences are inter-subjective. That is, two being's (e.g. mother and baby; teacher and student; therapist and client) are constantly affecting each other's experience (internal and external) on a moment-by-moment basis. We are influenced by the other and the other is influenced by us. Hence, we are co-creating each other in a constantly evolving and dissolving relational flow.

Third important point: Our "self" is shaped by what we make of our relational world and what our relational world makes of us.

In our early years, our self develops because of the quality of our attachment relationships. In the beginning, we require our caregivers to assist in regulating our physiological, neurobiological and emotional/psychological states. If our caregivers do this in a "good enough" way, our brain and developing self can optimally grow. If however, our caregivers are NOT "good enough", our brain and developing self is required to cope with a level of stress which it literally cannot manage. This stress has a major negative impact on the growth of our brain and our developing self.

Fourth important point: The quality of our attachment relationships affects our growing brain and developing self.

Neuroscience informs us that we probably don't have a single unitary "self" but have sub-systems, which include; a right-brain implicit self and a left-brain explicit self.[29] Our implicit self is probably more unconscious, while our explicit self is more conscious. Although there is not a definite demarcation between these selves, they do develop at different points in time and process information in their own unique way.

Our right-brain implicit self is the earliest to form and is related to the non-verbal, emotional, symbolic, inter-connected, intuitive, holistic and not fully graspable part of us.[30] On the other-hand, our left-brain explicit self, forms later and is related to the verbal, analytical, explainable and consciously aware part of us.[31] These sub-systems work in conjunction: Firstly, the right-brain implicit self somatically, emotionally and symbolically receives and experiences information, which the left-brain explicit self is then able to make sense of and verbalise. Although we often think this explicit self is dominant, as it is the one which speaks, it is the right-brain implicit self which is truly dominant in human existence.[32]

Fifth important point: Our right-brain implicit self is central to our human existence.

Like the undertow in a current determines the movement of water, the right-brain implicit self determines the flow of our human experience. Psychologically speaking then, it is our somatic, emotional, symbolic, relational, creative and intuitive capacities which dominate our experience as a *real* human being. Once we have this as our bedrock, the left-brain explicit self is then also obviously important, as it allows us to make sense of, reflect upon and communicate our human experience.

Development of Self: Part II

We are born as a *being* with a potential self. Our potential self is thought, by some scholars, to be unified or whole in the beginning.[33] Our in-utero experience and birth will affect such wholeness, as will the ensuing relational environment we are born into.

Upon birth, we do not have a "self" and cannot be called a "person" in the psychological sense yet. For the development of our self, or the becoming of a person, is largely dependent upon the quality of (emotional) relationship we have with our primary attachment figures, particularly in the first few years of our life. It is this relationship which allows our potential self (or what I will call "natural being and aliveness"[e]) to develop form, structure, organisation and coherence. This relational process is essentially what may be termed the development of self.

If the quality of this relationship is "good enough", then our "natural being and aliveness" starts to become coherent. Here's an example of how this relational process occurs. Let's say, in a spontaneous gesture of joy, a baby wiggles their body, kicks their legs and waves their arms, while smiling and expressing a happy gurgling sound. Their caregiver experiences this and in an attuned response feels joy, shimmies their body, smiles with the baby and then verbally makes a happy gurgling noise too. Importantly, the

---

[e] "Natural being and aliveness" is our essential aliveness as a human being. See box titled "Terminology" for a description of this term and how I am using it.

intensity of the caregiver's response is matched to the *intensity* displayed by the natural spontaneous gesture of the baby. Through the "natural being and aliveness" of the baby being seen, understood and responded to in a "good enough" way, the baby experiences coherence. Since their "natural being and aliveness" is experienced as *real* by another person, the baby becomes to experience themselves as real. Thus a "good enough" relationship allows a baby to remain *whole* while becoming a *real* person.

Something different occurs however, when the quality of the primary attachment relationship is NOT "good enough". Let's take the above example again, of a baby joyfully wriggling their body, smiling and gurgling. This time however, the caregiver remains unmoved and perhaps stares blankly or frowns at the baby. Here, there is incongruence between the expression and needs of the baby's "natural being and aliveness" and their caregiver's relational response.

This is a stressful dilemma for the infant. Their natural needs and internal experience are at odds with the external relational response, which they depend upon for survival and cohesion. In this situation, the baby will experience distress, which will result in incoherence and disconnection, if not repaired.

An infant is unable to manage this level of distress. Since they are fully dependent on their caregivers for survival, do not have the brain mechanisms (e.g. neo-cortex) to manage such stress and cannot understand it is the relational environment which is the problem, they have only one option; negate the expression and needs of their "natural being and aliveness" and adapt to the caregiver's failed response. In this example, if such a failure is consistently repeated without repair, the baby, unable to manage such levels of distress will eventually stop trying to *communicate* with their caregiver. Their wiggling and joyous gurgling will cease, and they will become still and unmoved. This disconnection from their "natural being and aliveness" means the infant becomes divided from their *realness*.

When the infant's "natural being and aliveness" is negated, this part of them becomes inaccessible for further growth. This real and human part of the baby is therefore stuck and frozen, unable to be included in the developing self. The infant must continue to grow, but it is now with a self *depleted* of this part of their "natural being and aliveness". Furthermore, the infant has no choice but to adapt and comply with the failed response of their caregiver. This results in the development of what has been called a "false self".[f] This false self protects the baby from feeling the extreme distress (e.g. terror, rage, grief) of not having the "good enough" attachment relationship to depend upon for survival and growth.

Terminology

Natural Being and Aliveness
"Natural being and aliveness" is not easily defined with words and is something which is best understood experientially. Given this limitation of words, I will do my best to give a description. This however, needs to be considered as a general pointer, rather than as definitive.

Overall, it is our essential aliveness and all that this encompasses. Natural, organic, spontaneous, creative and authentic in expression. It is best described using metaphors drawn from the natural world (e.g. plants, ocean), rather than metaphors based on machines or computers. Words such as "life-force", "spark",

---

[f] Again, see box titled, "Terminology" for a definition of this term.

"essence" and "spirit" also point us in the right direction.

It is the seed of our *realness* as a human being. Like a seed inherently needs soil, water and sun to grow, our "natural being and aliveness" needs attachment (relationship/intimacy) and individuation (separation/solitude), to allow it to become coherent and take form.

Our body is the vessel or container in which it is held and expressed. Thus, our breathing, beating heart and gut feelings can act as conduits to touch it. Finally, our somatic, symbolic, emotional, relational, intuitive and creative capacities arise from here.

I will generally use the words "natural being and aliveness" or "being and aliveness". Sometimes I will just use *being, aliveness* or *realness,* depending on which feels more fitting at the time. I will also very occasionally, use "heart and soul" when such a description seems fitting.

Self

The self arises at the interface between our "natural being and aliveness" and the (socio-cultural) relationships in which we belong.

Whole (Real) Self

When self emerges from "natural being and aliveness" it remains whole and may be said to be real. This self comes into being through "good enough" relational environments (with people who are *whole* themselves). In the first few years of life, the whole self emerges and develops when the caregivers attune and respond adequately to the "natural being and aliveness" of the infant and child. Through this "good enough" relationship, the "natural being and aliveness" remains whole, becomes coherent and develops form (i.e. a self) which is felt to be real.

I will generally use the word "wholeness" or "whole self" to describe this, as I like the sense of unity and connection it portrays. Feel free to use "real self", if you prefer.

Depleted/False Self

In the first few years of life, a depleted/false self will emerge and develop when the caregivers DO NOT attune and respond adequately to the "natural being and aliveness" of the infant and child. This results in a self which is disconnected from "natural being and aliveness", thus it is depleted and experienced as false. "False self" is a term first used by Donald Winnicott to describe a self which comes about to manage the failures of a "not good enough" relational environment. Since the infant and child must adapt to their caregivers' failures, a "false self" develops.

I will use the term "depleted/false self". I like the word *depleted* as it describes the consequence of the disconnection from "natural being and aliveness". Thus, this self feels exhausted, tired, empty and literally depleted. I will also continue to use the term *false* as this illuminates the adaptive and compliant nature of this self. If the term "false" feels somewhat negative, please use a word which resonates with you (e.g. functional, conditioned, learnt, ideal, compliant, adapted or coping self).

Whole vs. Depleted/False Self

If our early relational environment was "good enough", we probably have a greater sense of fullness and security. Our self was able to develop in connection with our "natural being and aliveness", so we feel more whole rather than depleted and more real rather than false. See diagram 1.

Self which arises is basically whole

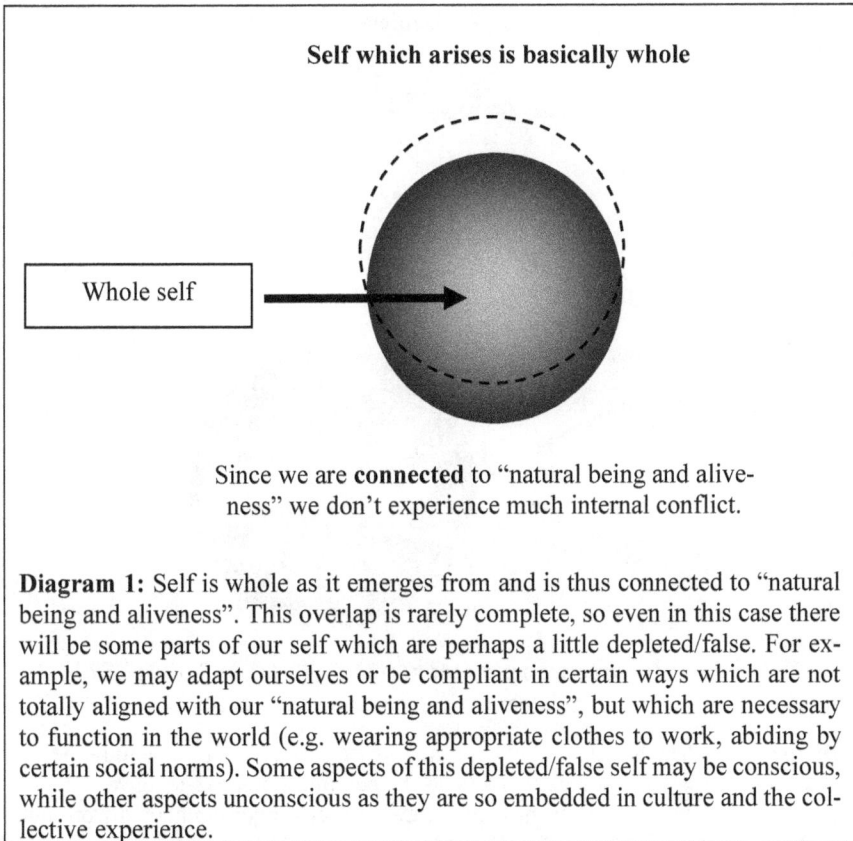

Whole self →

Since we are **connected** to "natural being and aliveness" we don't experience much internal conflict.

Diagram 1: Self is whole as it emerges from and is thus connected to "natural being and aliveness". This overlap is rarely complete, so even in this case there will be some parts of our self which are perhaps a little depleted/false. For example, we may adapt ourselves or be compliant in certain ways which are not totally aligned with our "natural being and aliveness", but which are necessary to function in the world (e.g. wearing appropriate clothes to work, abiding by certain social norms). Some aspects of this depleted/false self may be conscious, while other aspects unconscious as they are so embedded in culture and the collective experience.

If our early relational environment was NOT "good enough" then a different situation occurs. We may feel partly depleted, empty and insecure in our self. This is because parts of our self are disconnected from our "natural being and aliveness", which means we are left with a depleted self. In addition, since we had to comply with the failures of our caregivers, parts of our self are false. Furthermore, because of this split in our wholeness of self, we experience inner (unconscious) conflict; with parts of us wanting to be embodied and expressed, while other parts try to shut this down. See diagram 2.

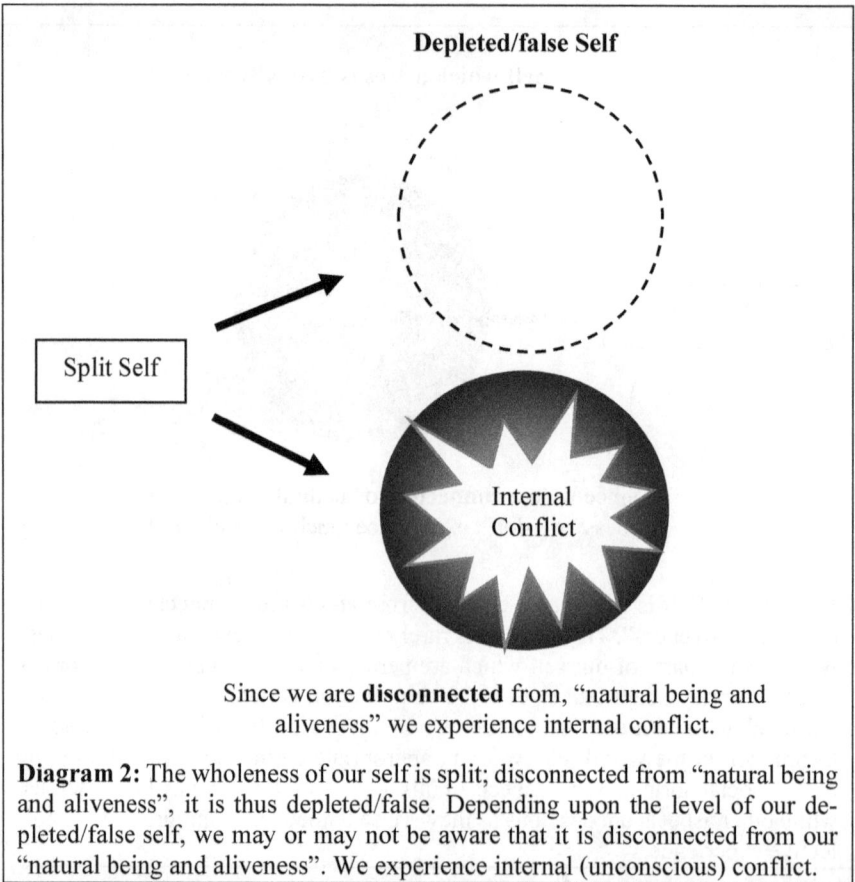

Depleted/false Self

Split Self

Internal Conflict

Since we are **disconnected** from, "natural being and aliveness" we experience internal conflict.

Diagram 2: The wholeness of our self is split; disconnected from "natural being and aliveness", it is thus depleted/false. Depending upon the level of our depleted/false self, we may or may not be aware that it is disconnected from our "natural being and aliveness". We experience internal (unconscious) conflict.

It is inevitable, when growing up, that some misattunement and thus conflict occurs for every infant and child. So as adults, we may all have parts of us which are a bit depleted/false. Perhaps then we may think more in terms of a continuum, rather than a dichotomy of either wholeness or depletion/falseness. Thus, there may be aspects of both flow (i.e. connection) and rigidity/chaos (i.e. disconnection), between our "natural being and aliveness" and the self which arises. The nature of this relationship then, is complex and individual.

In short, when there is more flow and connection in this relationship, our self is more whole, and we have less of a depleted/false self. As such, we are more psychologically resilient. That is, our self is both flexible and strong. We exist and are a creative and spontaneous being.[34]

However, when there is greater rigidity/chaos and disconnection in this relationship, our self is more split, and we live from a more prominent depleted/false self. As such, we experience greater psychological difficulty. That is, our self tends to be more inflexible, chaotic and/or fragile. At the most extreme, we are like a puppet, and do not psychologically exist as a *real* person.

"THE HEALTHY PERSONALITY DOES NOT FEEL TO BE IN TWO PARTS, ONE HIDING FROM THE WORLD WITHIN THE OTHER, BUT WHOLE, ALL OF A PIECE, AND ACTIVE AS A UNITY."
Harry Guntrip (1968). In *Schizoid Phenomena, Object Relations and the Self,* P,63.

Internal (Unconscious) Conflict

If our attachment relationships, early in life, were "not good enough", we had to adapt ourselves around these failures. This meant, we had to negate parts of our "natural being and aliveness" and develop a self which was compliant to our caregivers' failures.[g] Even though this protected us and allowed us to survive, it also created an inherent problem or conflict in us.

Basically, it's like we grow up to be an adult, but with parts of us alienated within our unconscious. Since these alienated parts have not been provided with the nourishment they need to grow, they remain undeveloped and so often have an infantile or childlike *emotional* sense to them.

These infantile and childlike parts are our realness as a human being. Even though they may now be inaccessible (or unconscious), they never completely disappear, and today still seek to be included in our wholeness.

But the problem is, because our early relational environment failed to embrace these parts of us, we have also learnt these parts of us "cannot" or "should not" be included in our whole self. So now as an adult, we continue to negate and treat these parts of us, in the same "not good enough" way we learnt growing up. So even though these infantile and childlike parts want to grow, develop

---

[g] What we negate and how we adapt is specific to us and our situation. This is partially dependent on what phase of development we are in and thus what our specific needs are at that time. This is the major topic of PART II of this book.

and be included in our wholeness, as an adult we often feel critical towards them and resist acknowledging they even exist in us.

This is the dilemma: On one side, we intuitively feel our wholeness as a human being and yearn to embody and be this. This includes embodying all our infantile and childlike parts, so they can grow and develop as part of our whole self. On the other side, since we have implicitly taken in what is okay and not okay to be, we have certain ideas about how we "should be" as a person. This generally does not include our infantile and childlike parts, so once again they are negated and remain alienated and disconnected from our wholeness.

The legacy of this conflict is that we feel a tug-of-war occurring inside of us. One part of us wants to be expressed, while another part fearing this expression tries to shut it down. Here are some examples. A part of me feels sad, but another part thinks I should be strong and not cry. A part of me wants to express anger, but another part of me thinks it's not nice to get angry. A part of me wants to just be, but another part is afraid if it doesn't keep pushing it will cease to exist. A part of me wants to express an opinion, but another part feels anxious when this opinion differs from others.[h]

This internal struggle is difficult to manage. To try and feel better, we often continue to force ourselves to be who we *think* we should or shouldn't be, while disowning certain feelings and experiences.

---

[h] For more examples of internal conflict, see box titled "Other Examples of Internal Conflict".

Other Examples of Internal Conflict

- I yearn for more intimacy in my life, but feel suffocated and trapped when I get close to someone.

- Even though I have achieved much in my life, I experience a niggling feeling of inadequacy.

- I feel irritated when someone asks me for something, but cannot say no.

- Even though I need help, I find it almost impossible to ask for it.

- I am extremely responsible in my life, but have one habit which is unusually irresponsible (e.g. drink driving, having unprotected promiscuous sex, road rage).

- I feel committed in my relationship, but am having an affair.

- I feel drained and tired by all the tasks I do, but cannot stop being busy.

What this Means for Us Now

S ince our internal conflicts began many years ago and occur fairly unconsciously, we might think they don't impact us anymore. Unfortunately, this is not the case. Such a war against ourselves, robs us of much needed energy, resilience and internal resources, as well as keeping hostage our wholeness as a human being.

Maybe we can imagine it like a computer virus running in the background, messing with our system, while using up all our data and power. It takes a lot of psychological energy to fight the parts of us that naturally want to be expressed. It also takes a lot of energy to try and hide or adapt the parts of ourselves we think we shouldn't feel, secretly think are wrong or experience as shameful. These parts may include some of our infantile and childlike emotions, flaws, vulnerabilities, sensitivities or desires. Much of our power is used up in this struggle, causing us to feel tired and strained.

The way our self became to be, what it is today, in many ways is what enabled us to survive in our earliest years.[35] Consequently, as an adult, we are invested in keeping it the way it is, even though it may cause us suffering. Furthermore, this way of being is familiar to us; it is who we experience ourselves to be, as well as how we make sense of and function in the world.

Even so, making positive changes to our self by becoming more whole is possible.[i] This possibility is exemplified by what neuro-science calls neural plasticity. This basically means our brain and self is not hardwired, but can grow and change with new experiences.

To what extent, we may become whole, is somewhat uncertain. There is a term in the psychological literature called "earned secure", where someone who has not had a secure attachment works to eventually change their attachment style similar to that of a secure. This earned secure is not the same as the secure, but perhaps on par. To be poetic, maybe earned security is like the vase which has been cracked, and through the loving art of Kintsugi and wisdom of Wabi-sabi has been repaired to wholeness again.

This earned secure attachment is dependent on the factors discussed in the previous and ensuing sections on repair. It is also perhaps, dependent on other factors which are not as easily explained and that pertain more to the complexity inherent in any type of organic system. Generally though, the good news is, if we are sincerely dedicated to the work of becoming more whole, change is possible.[36]

In general, if we have had a secure attachment growing up, this psychological work will probably not be too difficult or enduring. However, if our attachment tends towards insecurity (i.e. avoidant or ambivalent), then this work will require significant effort from us. It will also take time and we will probably need the assistance of a professional therapist. Finally, in the case of a disorganised/disorientated attachment, this may be our life's work and often becomes our most meaningful purpose.

---

[i] This process is the essence of PART II.

L et's stop for a quick check in. If some of the details so far seem a bit much, that's okay.

The main thing to get is this: we develop and grow through our relational experiences. This is particularly pertinent in the first few years of life and then continues throughout our life, until the very end. If our experiences of relationships in the beginning of our life were "good enough", we have a bit of a head start on this journey of healing and becoming whole. If however, our experiences were NOT "good enough", then we probably have some catching-up to do.

We learn about and understand our self, the other and the world, through our experiences of relationship.

The Process of Repair

It might be useful now, before we step onto the main road, to illuminate the general process of repair to becoming more whole. I say general, as the specifics of this process will be fleshed out in the next section, PART II of this book. So in general, the process of repair involves; grieving what we *missed*, feeling and moving through the pains of growing-up, letting go of the ways we have adapted ourselves, and coming home to a more conscious, embodied and whole experience of our self.

So firstly, *missed* means, when growing-up there was something which wasn't there for us (i.e. absent or not enough) and/or there was something which felt too much and overwhelming. This *something* is usually related to connection and relationship with a person, rather than an object or thing. Unless we were malnourished and living in poverty, which means we also missed some of the necessities of life (e.g. food, shelter, medical care and education).

Sometimes what we missed is evident. For example, we may remember being physically punished (e.g. hit, grabbed or pushed) when we said, "No", to one of our parents. Here, we missed a parent who can manage their own emotions (i.e. anger) and tolerate our increasing independence and development of a separate sense of self. Alternatively, perhaps our parent expected us to be independent and self-sufficient too quickly, and so we missed a parent who is comfortable with someone being dependent and needing them.

In other circumstances however, it is very difficult to identify what we missed. Since we didn't have it growing-up, it feels normal not to have it, so we probably don't consciously think there was something wrong. In this case, we might only know we missed something as a by-product of other things. For example, we might experience persistent feelings of fear, sadness, grief, aloneness or anger, which don't always relate to our current external circumstance. Alternatively, we might discover what we missed when someone in our life provides it for us, and we notice how unfamiliar it feels to be given what we rarely or never got. For example, if someone is kind to us and we feel uncomfortable, suspicious, sad or even angry about it. Finally, we may become aware of what we missed, when we observe other people getting something and we become sad, angry or envious.

In moving through the pains of growing-up, we begin to experience the parts of ourselves which needed to be hidden, abandoned, cut off and negated. We may get in touch with intense anger, rage, sadness, grief, despair, shame, heart-break, abandonment, hopelessness, helplessness and fear. Our work is to gradually integrate these negated emotional parts into an embodied and whole self. This means, slowly and over time, we can *be with* the full range of our emotional experience.

In letting go of the ways we have adapted ourselves, we acknowledge the ways our adaptation and compliance was necessary for our survival. We begin to understand that now as an adult we do not need this false self-survival mechanism anymore. Finally, we recognise the ways our false self may have inadvertently betrayed our heart and soul. In grieving this betrayal of our self, we are moved to live more centred in our authenticity.

In this process of repair, we work to understand how we have been impacted from the failures in our early environment. This includes acknowledging our strength to survive and cultivating compassion for the wounded child within. In understanding our resultant strengths and limitations, we may then see and experience ourselves more honestly.

This process of repair is about reclaiming our wholeness. We reclaim our physical wholeness, feeling safe and at home in our body. We reclaim our vast array of feelings, our right to be fully alive and make our own choices. Most importantly, we reclaim the right to be our full, flawed, weird and wonderful self.

Repair must occur through relationship, for
it is relationship which heals.

Our sense of self is developed through our relational experiences.[37] Since it is through relationship we come to be, the work of repair of our self also needs to occur through this avenue. I emphasise this, as some of us will have the tendency to read this book and try to work out a solution on our own. Even if this is done with great earnestness and commitment, to heal and become whole, we eventually need to bring this work into relationship. I will outline three major reasons why this is necessary and beneficial.

Firstly, all life exists in connection. All things arise in inter-dependence upon something else. For example, fire requires fuel and oxygen; without one of these it will cease to exist. Relationship then is a fundamental truth of all life, including us.

Secondly, we humans are relational beings. We come into this world hard-wired for connection.[38] This is fundamental to our growth. As an infant and child, the development of our sense of self is achieved through relationship. Basically, we can only grow and mature as a human being in connection with another human being. If our relationships in our early years were "not good enough", we were probably not able to grow and develop into the wholeness we are. Consequently, we will need to have a *felt* experience of a "good enough" relationship, if we want to work towards repairing our wholeness.

A "good enough" relationship, whether therapeutic or personal, provides us with *enough* safety, presence, understanding, kindness, freedom and boundaries, as well as some frustration, disappointment and reality testing. If this is what we missed in our early years, this relationship will allow us to contact those parts of us we have negated, allowing us to encounter our joy and pain; our wholeness as human beings. Within this relationship and over time, we express and experience what we were not able to express and experience with our early caregivers, thus allowing us to let go of the ways we adapt ourselves. When we are psychologically held by this person (i.e. feel safe, heard, known and valued), we in turn learn to embrace our whole self, including all the feelings and thoughts tucked away in our unconscious. In this way, we can *be with* ALL that we are, having had the relational experience of another *being with* ALL that we are.

The third reason we do this repair work in relationship is to shed light on our *blind spots*. If we do not have someone else to "check-in" with, we will probably approach this work in habitual ways. This may not always be effective and perhaps could even compound the problem. For example, if we tend to negate our feelings and focus more on our intellect, we will probably employ this bias when doing the repair work I am suggesting here. If we approach this type of work with our intellect alone, we will not get very far. We might gain an excellent cerebral understanding of it, but that is all. Intellectual understanding, on its own, does not make us whole. Alternatively, we might tend to blame other people for what is occurring for us. If we continue to do this, we avoid looking more deeply within our self; the antithesis of discovering our full human beingness. We will not necessarily see these habitual patterns or blind spots in ourselves. But when we do this work within relationship, the other person can observe and highlight them for us. It is beneficial if this person understands where we may be stuck; compassionately sees our blind spots, but does not collude with our blindness. Our self-awareness may then grow through this relationship.

We change, develop and grow through our
relational experiences.

Change Occurs Face to Face

Our connection to all of life is essential. This includes our interaction and relationship with others like us (i.e. humans) and all other species in our world (including animals, plants and minerals).

In our modern world, we spend a large amount of time interacting with inanimate objects, such as computers, the internet, mobile phones, television, etc. These objects may be useful, to do work, obtain information or maintain a link with people (especially if they do not live near us). But as far as our wellbeing is concerned, they add very little. We are embodied, relational and conscious beings, and so it is the connections we have with other living species which have the most significant impact on us.

Engaging in direct face-to-face relational experiences is essential for our wellbeing.[39] Remember, we are born with an innate need for connection, and we develop and grow through our relationships. An important part of this, is the total sensory experience occurring when two embodied beings interact with each other. That is, the energetic resonance, nuances of connection and aliveness of all our self, being engaged with all of the other. This energetic exchange occurs when two beings are face-to-face; it cannot be replicated via a computer screen.

In the field of neuroscience, this is called limbic resonance; where the limbic region of our brain releases certain neurochemicals essential for our wellbeing. This limbic resonance may be positive or negative. If we feel safe, seen and cared about by the other person, then our limbic region will release stress reducing neuro-chemicals, such as oxytocin. These chemicals affect our physical and psychological wellbeing in a positive and growth enhancing way.[40] If however, we feel unsafe, unseen and not cared about by the other person, our limbic region releases stress intensifying neu-rochemicals, such as cortisol, which negatively affect our health and wellbeing.[41] This may occur if we are bullied, harassed, ig-nored, used, humiliated, isolated, etc.

In a nutshell: we require positive limbic resonance for our phys-ical and psychological wellbeing. We get this from face-to-face in-teractions when we feel safe, seen and cared about. In our relationships then, it is wise to be discerning; maintaining connec-tions where we experience this, and limiting connections in which we don't.

If in growing up we lacked these nourishing (limbic) connections, particularly with other human beings, but also with animals and our natural environment, our bricks of experience will be impov-erished. In the same way, if our relational experiences felt harmful to us, our bricks will be damaged in some way. If then we want to repair the bricks of our self, we need to do it through the direct engagement in nourishing relational experiences, rather than through inanimate objects such as computers or books.

You might then wonder, why I am writing a book to get this message across. As although there is some living element to it, that is me the author, it is still largely an activity you are doing without direct relational experience, especially if you are reading it alone. This is a good question and my answer to it is this. I like to write, so this is my way to get this information to you. I have also often relied on books for assistance in my own development. And even though I use them much less now as I understand there is more *juice* in direct relational experiences, books have allowed me, in a very safe way, to begin this exploration.

This is my hope for you also; to use this book as a starting point. We cannot read something on our own and directly change. Information integrated through this way, can influence us, encourage us, point us in the right direction and provide us with some helpful hints. But if we do not step beyond this, it will remain as mere intellectual information. Intellectual information, on its own, does not change us; direct (relational) experience does.

PART II

The Road Ahead

A large part of this book is about illuminating what we now require to grow, psychologically, if in our earliest years of development we didn't get what we needed to become whole. Since our first several years are typically considered to be the most influential, I've divided this time into four phases, based upon general agreement in the psychological literature.[j] These phases may act as a framework to reflect upon our developmental needs. If we did not get these needs met in a "good enough" way, we probably have some unfinished psychological business to attend to.

In each phase, I will briefly examine our developmental needs and then discuss the type of issues which may arise for us, as an adult, if they were not met in a "good enough" way. Within this framework, I also illuminate a path of repair, so we may complete our unfinished psychological growth, heal and become whole.

This is not meant as a definite or rigid analysis. Each of us is an individual and our life is more intricate, complex and mysterious than I am able to demonstrate in these phases. Hence, it is a framework, allowing us a start in understanding ourselves better, as well as illuminating a possible pathway for growth. Having a framework, like this, is especially useful when we find ourselves experiencing feelings or doing things which seem uncharacteristic of our usual self.

---

[j] See box on the following page titled "The 4 Phases in Brief".

The 4 Phases in Brief

Phase One: Safe and sound ground (conception/birth to 3-6 mths)
Basic ontological security; there is a place for me in this world. I
am welcome, I belong, I am safe and I am held in connection.

Phase Two: A solid and secure foundation (3-6 months to 15 mths)
Nourishment of needs; I can depend on you. My needs are okay, I
am supported, I have enough and I am satisfied.

Phase Three: A well-constructed house (15 months to 3-4 years)
Development of a separate self in relationship; it's okay to be me
with you. I am real, I am free to be me and I can be both vulnerable
and strong.

Phase Four: A Home (3-4 years to 6-7 years)
Love, Self-Expression, Sexuality and Competition; I am worthy. I
can be both competent and make mistakes, I am centred in being
and aliveness and my world of relationship becomes wider.

When we are growing up, we generally go from the first phase to
the final phase. It is important to note however, that there is fluidity
in these developmental phases. So rather than thinking about them
as four fixed and separate steps, perhaps see them more like four
pools of water; which have their own reservoir, but are also able to
flow in and out of each other.

When we are dealing with these phases as an adult, my sense is
our conscious awareness (although not totally linear) tends to work
from the fourth to the first. Everyone has probably heard the "in-
famous" onion metaphor, about unpeeling each layer until we

eventually arrive at our inner core. With the house metaphor uti-lised here, it is a similar process. So we might begin by looking at and understanding phase four initially, which may then lead us to investigate phase three, two and one respectively. For example, we start to become aware of some decor that isn't quite right, which then leads us to see that there are actually some construction prob-lems with the house itself. Then as we are looking more closely at how we see and navigate our worlds, we might notice these con-struction issues are caused by an unsteady foundation (if this is the case for us), and so on.

In saying this however, there is no need to solidify or think about this process too much, for again in reality it is quite fluid. Paying attention to our own experience is the most important thing, rather than adhering to an idea of how this process should be. As we stay with our subjective experience, taking one step at a time, the next step arises for us. If we can *trust* enough to do this, we will naturally progress through what we need to.

As you read through the four phases, you will probably sense which phases resonate with you and which ones don't. When I say resonate, I mean, when something triggers a reaction; either posi-tive or negative. Sometimes when it is a negative response, we tend to disown it and quickly move on. Be aware of this, as this may be the exact place you need to explore a little more.

You may also, at some points, have a vague feeling of not want-ing to read on. This halt could be illuminating a *stuck* point on your path. If you are serious about this journey, perhaps meander here for a while, become curious about what you're feeling and talk to someone about it. Such a stuck point can represent an opportunity for new growth; a bit like the first green shoot of a seedling pushing through the soil.

Suggestions for Reading

In reading PART II, it may be useful to initially read through all four phases, to get the general gist of the developmental sequence. Then you might like to pick the phase you are most drawn to and begin working in more detail at that level. This is one suggestion. Essentially though, each of you must feel it out for yourselves and do what works for you. Trust your own pace and process. At times you may skip, dance or run through it, while at other times you plod, dawdle or crawl.

Certain parts of this section may be beneficial to some, while others find quite different parts useful. I trust each of you will take what you need. If you need to take a break away from it, you may always come back to it later. If you want to compare it to other sources and get a second opinion, I encourage this.

Most of all, I hope each one of you finds a person you feel safe with, to share and talk about your experience as you proceed. It is beneficial if this other person wants to understand, support and perhaps even share this process you are undertaking. If some of you cannot think of someone you trust to talk about this "stuff" with, it is vital at some point to find someone (e.g. a registered therapist) you may grow to feel safe with.

Remember, this book is a guide and source of encouragement. But if you read it and then put it back on the shelf to gather dust, you will not get the *juice* you need from it. The juice here is bringing this information into your life and relationships. Talk about it, experiment with new ways of being and perhaps even play with the ideas presented here.

Down the Rabbit Hole We Go...

One day I was speaking to a friend of mine who was going through a difficult time. She'd been feeling down.

"It's okay to take a peek right?"

"You could even go all the way." I replied with a hint of cheekiness.

She was talking about the trepidation of entering the rabbit hole of her internal world. This is what this section is about; the journey into our emotional labyrinth.

If we want to heal, feel whole and live as fully as possible, we need to do more than just peek down our rabbit hole. We need to get amongst it, get down and dirty and feel it out.

Perhaps you might like to put your seatbelt on as it'll be a bit of a ride. Are you ready?

Phase One

Safe and Sound Ground

(Conception/Birth to 3-6 months)

In our metaphor of building a house, this beginning period is akin to the type of land the foundation is laid upon. Indeed, the first and most essential consideration is to ask whether the land is favourable to hold a stable and secure base for the house to rest upon. If it isn't, a builder and engineer will reinforce it until it is ready, for they understand it is simply ludicrous to lay a foundation on unsteady land.

Basic Ontological Security

There is a place for me in this world

I am welcome | I belong | I am safe | I am held in connection

A newborn coming into this world is extremely vulnerable. Initially, birth is a traumatic event for these conscious beings, who've been (in most situations) protected and receiving what they need for forty weeks in their mother's womb. Even though the actual process of birthing can be difficult, it is the entry into this world which is sudden and shocking. What we have grown familiar with as adults is very different to the womb environment infants are accustomed to.

The womb for some babies is not always one hundred percent conducive to their needs however. Some may not receive the general nutrients for adequate growth. Others may be affected by the adverse emotions passed on by the mother, because of various pre-existing or current environmental difficulties she needs to contend with. For example, lack of support, excessive stress or unresolved grief, trauma and depression. Indeed, if the mother is significantly distressed, the developing embryo is also taking this in as part of their experience, particularly in the final trimester of pregnancy. Consequently, the mother's well-being has an important impact on the developing infant's brain and nervous system.[42]

At birth, newborns are confronted by an environment, which compared to the womb, relatively speaking, is harsh. Rather than a warm fluid to surround them, there is unfamiliar air and space. Depending on the type of birth and who is in attendance, there are probably loud noises, bright lights and someone handling them in perhaps a non-gentle way. Although coming into this world is experienced as a shock, it is obviously necessary. With some attention to providing a calm and soothing environment for both the mother and the baby, the effects of this distress may be lessened.

*At birth, the baby, although physically sepa-
rate from its mother, is still totally dependent
on her for survival and growth.*

With advances in the neurosciences, we now know the newborn's brain and nervous system is not fully developed. Even at nine months of age, post birth, the brain has only grown to 50% of its adult capacity.[43] Consequently, before babies begin to crawl, attachment to a physically and emotionally present person is essential for their survival and growth. This is beautifully described by Sharon Heller[k] as follows:

"Our silent and most potent language, touch, is the medium through which parent and infant communicate and become attached, each tender touch strengthening the bond between them. It nurtures our infant's psychological growth; stimulates their physical and mental growth; assures smoothness of physiological functions like breathing, heart rate and digestion; enhances their self-concept, body awareness, and sexual identity; boosts immune system; and even enhances the grace and stability of their movement." (S.Heller p, 5)

Thus, the physical and emotional relationship with the primary attachment figure is essential for the infant's survival. Physical touch and emotional presence assist the infant with the regulation of their physiology, such as hunger, temperature, sleep, hormone levels, immune and cardiovascular function.[44] It also provides the infant with the essential psychological needs of safety, welcome, belonging, emotional regulation and connection.[45] The need for

---

[k] See, Heller, S. (1997). The Vital Touch: How Intimate Contact with Your baby Leads To Happier, Healthier Development. Holt Paperbacks.

this in infancy is further reinforced, when we understand that it is only around two or three years of age when a child begins to learn to do these functions for themselves.

The brain of a baby is still in its very early stages of development, and does not have the anatomy (namely, hippocampus or neocortex) to make sense of their environment. The hippocampus, responsible for modulating and making contextual sense of our environment, comes on line around two or three years of age. Before this, experience and learning register in the amygdala (the emotional centre of the brain) and hence are not contextualised but laid down globally as somatic emotional memories.[46] This means a baby literally experiences their environment in a very raw and unfiltered way.

The attachment figure and relational environment is then also taken in wholly, by the newborn, without filtering and with limited sense of difference between the two. So if the attachment person and environment is calm, warm and loving, this will also be the newborn's experience. If however, they are anxious, angry or cold, this will be what is felt by the baby.

These experiences are laid down at an implicit and primitive level in the infant's developing brain and nervous system. This is the bedrock for the infant's developing right-brain implicit self.

This type of scientific knowledge allows us to be aware of the essential requirement of relationship as the cornerstone of physical and psychological growth of every infant. Indeed, we would consider it ludicrous to expect a baby to begin walking in their first several months of life, and so it is the same regarding their ability to make sense of and manage their physiological and psychological needs.

> *The attachment to a secure, stable and*
> *emotionally available other is of primary*
> *importance. This is not an optional extra, but*
> *an essential survival requirement for the infant.*

It is now regarded as essential that the newborn attaches securely to (at least) one person. This means, their felt experience is of *somatically knowing* they are held safely and securely in the arms, heart and mind of another.

Since the mother has carried the baby for forty weeks, so an attachment in most cases has already begun, and is usually the one that feeds him or her, it probably makes sense for the mother to be the primary attachment figure in the beginning. If for some reason she is unable to do this, then it is essential the baby is cared for by another constant, safe and present person.

An infant, in this phase, requires their first attachment figure to be what Donald Winnicott refers to as "devoted". Essentially, this caregiver[1] needs to be totally available to meet her baby's physical and emotional needs. To do this, she needs to be well herself, so she can be attuned and respond when her baby requires her. She also needs an adequate amount of support in her environment (e.g. a partner, family or friends); people who can take care, protect and support her while she does the important task of nurturing. Finally, it is important she not have too many other competing demands on her time or external stresses in her life, which interfere with her ability to take care of her newborn. [m]

---

[1] For ease of personal pronoun use, I will use *she* and *her*; in the assumption that the mother is generally the primary attachment figure in the first several weeks. If this isn't your situation, use the pronouns which best fit for you.

[m] These ideas about the care of an infant are taken from Donald Winnicott.

Most caregivers are devoted to their baby, providing enough holding and support for them to feel welcomed and safe in this new and unfamiliar world. In this way, the newborn maintains some illusion of non-separateness, enabling them to comfortably continue their extremely rapid growth through the first several months of life. Even though the direction of psychological growth and maturity is to understand oneself as a separate person in relationship to others, it is essential this realisation occur slowly and at the developmentally appropriate time (i.e. beginning in phase 2, peaking in phase 3 and culminating in phase 4).

It is therefore critical, both in the womb and several weeks after birth, babies are wrapped in a physical, emotional and mental sense of safety and security. A good illustration of this is a baby kangaroo in its mother's pouch.

To come into psychological existence, the baby requires physical and emotional connection to their attachment figure.

If the newborn is held and welcomed, physically, emotionally and mentally, it will grow to have what R.D. Laing[47] called "ontological security". This security is a very deep sense that one exists, belongs in this world and can trust life. It is a feeling of *being* and of *existing* as a person; grounded to earth, embodied, connected and welcomed to the human tribe.

If however, the attachment relationship is significantly compromised at this time, the newborn infant will be overwhelmed by their inability to manage on their own. Hence, a lack of attachment or serious breaches in attachment (without repair) at this time, is experienced as a life or death survival issue for the baby.

In this case, terror and overwhelm is implicitly embodied as their first experience of life. The nervous system and amygdala register this danger and prime the body for survival. The newborn physically cannot fight or flee, but only freeze. Since it is untenable to exist with such a constant experience of fright, the baby is forced to withdraw from their psychic existence. Withdrawing, allows them to survive; physically present but psychologically absent.

In this instance, the baby is without ontological security. They have begun their life experiencing the world as dangerous, terrifying and a struggle between life and death. Tragically, their legacy begins with "ontological insecurity" [n] and the fear of annihilation imprinted in their bodily unconscious.

To have this occur, so early, is a profound tragedy and a severe limitation for further emotional and social growth. Although the baby has physically survived, the psyche is now not present for ongoing development. The potential self has disappeared, before it's had a chance to come into existence.

The Legacy
In this early phase of development, we need to be welcomed into a secure and safe relational environment. It is essential we have an attachment figure who holds us physically and emotionally with their body, heart and mind.

If this was the case for us, we will now feel a sense of ontological security, where we experience a basic confidence, continuity and trust about our existence in the world. We feel embodied, safe, welcomed and that we belong with the people, groups and communities we are part of.

---

[n] A definition of this term is given further on in "The Legacy".

If however, we were not welcomed into this world and did not have a safe and available person to attach with in the first few months after birth, our legacy is "ontological insecurity". This is best described by Harry Guntrip[48] as follows:

"Ontological insecurity means insecurity to one's essential being and existence as a person, insecurity about one's ego-identity, the feeling of basic inadequacy in coping with life, and inability to maintain oneself as in any sense an equal in relationships with other people." (Guntrip, 1968)

We may experience issues of basic trust in life. Our sense of existing as a real person is tenuous, and we probably feel as if we are not welcomed and don't belong in the world. Finally, relationships may feel like a minefield. Our legacy then is one of feeling unreal and like an outsider, as if we don't belong to the human tribe and can expect only rejection from it.

What this Means for Us...Now

As an adult then, if we were born into an environment which was unwelcoming, unsafe and did not provide for our most basic needs, that is without a person to attach with securely, we have experienced a profound and irreplaceable loss. Our feelings of fear, rage, grief, despair and hopelessness, associated with this time in our life, may be buried very deeply inside. We may not even be aware these emotional states reside within us, until they are triggered by something which occurs in our life and relationships today.

Our healing process needs to begin with being safe, welcomed and connected; in our body, our environment and with at least one other person. It is essential we feel safe enough to reveal our inner world and explore the hidden parts of our self. Eventually, we will need to excavate our "natural being and aliveness" which has been buried deeply inside of us, to survive. In connection with our *aliveness* we may re-emerge into the world, with our whole self.

Basic Safety

We may not know what it feels like to have a sense of ontological security; a basic feeling of being okay in the world. Experiencing feelings of not belonging, not being welcomed and being alien to this earth. We may think we don't have a right to exist or there is something profoundly wrong with us, although if asked we probably wouldn't be able to say exactly what it is. We also might not feel safe in our body and escape it by dissociating from it (e.g. by being focused in our intellect, imagination or spirituality, through alcohol or drug use, or keeping very busy).

Our need now as an adult is to feel safe; to exist. This includes feeling safe with at least one other person, safe in our own body and safe within our external environment.[49]

It is possible we have never truly felt safe with another person. We may even, unwittingly, gravitate towards relationships which replay this very old infant wound of having to hide and withdraw from others. Perhaps we tend to stay in relationships where we remain somewhat disconnected or invisible. In this way we keep ourselves away from connection and intimacy. This allows us to manage the deep pain of terror, rage and despair associated with our early relational experience.

Although we did not receive the safety and security we needed from our caregivers, perhaps there was someone else, later in our life, who we felt some sense of safety with. This could be a relative (grandparent, aunt, uncle, cousin or sibling), teacher or sports coach. Maybe we had a friend whom we felt close to, or even an animal. If there was someone with whom we felt safe enough to be ourselves, we can remember this, knowing what it feels like to be with someone, without being afraid, hiding or feeling invisible. If however, we have never had this experience, it is important we discover it now.

For some of us, this relational safety will initially need to be found within the boundaries of a therapeutic relationship. If this still feels too scary for us right now, we can start slowly. Perhaps we begin by connecting with nature and animals. Then once we feel safe here, we move towards relating with another person.°

---

*When the warmth of human contact enters
the long-forgotten crevices of our heart, we are
touched by its loving presence.*

Over time, through relationship, we begin to understand we do not need to continuously hide, withdraw and be alone. We embody a feeling of connectedness and belonging, knowing there are people we can get close to without the fear of being abused, neglected or annihilated.

We will need time to familiarise ourselves with what it feels like to be safe and trust another. There may be many times when we think the opposite. Perceiving this person as unsafe and perhaps even dangerous, we may want to withdraw to feel okay. At these times it is healthy for us to bring our concerns to the person. We can then check the reality of our perceptions, see their response to our concerns and decide whether we will continue to take the risk of being in connection.

It is important we choose carefully the person we do this repair work with. Intuitively, we may know they are strong enough and

---

° See box titled, "But I Feel Scared When I Get Close to Someone!".

wise enough to walk beside us as we navigate the hidden and frozen emotional labyrinth inside us. If we have chosen someone to reveal our feelings to and the experience generally does not feel safe, this is NOT a sign we need to go into hiding again. It means we need to act and choose a different person to go through this process with.

This is a long road. It requires us to be with the warmth and closeness offered by another, without withdrawing or becoming invisible. It is this experience that allows us to heal and grow; knowing we have a right to exist. We too can be alive, feel safe, be held and belong.

But I Feel Scared When I Get Close to Someone!

Along the way, as you continue to read this book, you might ask yourself if you feel ready to try something more relationally direct. It can take a long time to have the courage to do this. It is understandable if you do not feel ready to share and do this work with another human being right now. This seems scary for some of us! There is no rush; take your time and set a pace which is comfortable for you.

You might want to begin slowly. Perhaps firstly by connecting to the earth; lying on the ground and experiencing what it feels like. You might also take some time to walk in the forest, swim in the ocean, dig in your garden or lie in the sun like a lizard. You might then feel drawn to being with the different animal species in your environment, feeling what it is like to connect and commune with each. Perhaps you are drawn to a specific animal (e.g. dog, cat, horse) and so you spend some time around this being.

Eventually you might become curious about connecting with

another human, like yourself. Engaging in a therapeutic relationship could be a way for you to safely experience this connection.
The professional boundaries of this relationship means it is more
likely you will have an experience of safety here, particularly as
these boundaries are bound by an ethical framework of doing no
harm.

You will need to allow yourself time and space to become familiar with how it feels to be with another person, without the
worry of having to brace yourself for danger. Stepping into this
unknown will feel uncomfortable and a little scary, but if you have
chosen the right person it will not generally feel dangerous or unsafe. This difference is something you will gradually learn to decipher and discern for yourself. One way to do this is to bring your
concerns to the person and notice how they respond. If they are
unable to listen to you, take your concerns seriously, become angry
at you or dismiss what you say, this is NOT a good sign. If they
take the time to listen, hear you and respond with some understanding of your concerns, this is a good sign. You may not always get
the outcome you want, but in the process, you will have felt seen
and heard.

It will feel *risky* to become close to someone. Especially if you
are more used to feeling afraid of those you are close to. Feeling
safe with closeness will probably be a new experience. And like
anything which is unfamiliar, it will have a few bumps along the
road before you become more at ease with it. It may take some
time to get used to. It might even take years to become close to
someone, so be gentle with yourself and know you can go as slow
or fast as is comfortable for you.

Real Relationships

We cannot do this journey alone.

As an infant, we were not able to remain connected with our "being and aliveness" and have someone hold us, soothe us and essentially be the wiser and stronger person. So learning to trust our *aliveness* is okay and can be experienced with another person, will take time.

We are probably so familiar with our inner world being unseen and unacknowledged, that we expect others won't see us and won't understand us. We might think, if we express our feelings of anger, grief or fear, we will annihilate ourselves or annihilate the other person. So we hold our emotional world tightly inside. We may also, unconsciously, experience our need for human contact as overwhelming, and thus fear being overwhelmed ourselves or overwhelming the other with our needs. Consequently, we also keep our desire for relationship secretly inside. Trusting it is okay to show our whole self to someone, (i.e. feelings, needs and desires), will be one of the most courageous chasms we cross.

If our initial attachment experience was unsafe, painful, overwhelming, intrusive, cold or neglectful, we may have great difficulty in close relationships as adults, particularly intimate ones. We might continuously withdraw into our shell, feeling deeply alone, but safe (to a certain degree). Or we maintain a connection to others, but in a shallow way, to starve off the terror of annihilation.

> *We might experience relationships in a "as if" way, not feeling truly connected with anyone.*[50]

We probably wonder what this "so called life" is all about; not quite getting it. Feeling on the outer, we are an observer of life, rather than a true participant. We think we prefer it this way.

Staying on the edges we feel safer, as to be involved means the risk of being hurt again. Indeed, when there is an inkling or sign of this, our immediate strategy is to withdraw, hide and perhaps only superficially participate and relate.

> *We might live most of our life in a type of limbo land, never having fully arrived. Perhaps even sensing some important part of us is suspended in space or on another planet.*

We could alternate between feeling confused, unsure and somewhat alien in this world, to feeling angry, superior and think relationships are over-rated. Silently mocking the mundane lives of others, we think we are above it all; not subjected to the monotony of ordinary human feelings and relationships. However, when this defence of detachment and not needing others wears down, we feel an intense and deep longing for connection, which sometimes has an *unrequited love* feel to it.

We may also observe other people expressing themselves and engaging in relationship with little difficulty and thus feel different, odd, or that there is something wrong with us. Although there is nothing inherently wrong with us, we do experience a tricky dilemma when it comes to relating; closeness and intimacy feels scary and overwhelming, but so does too much distance and isolation. One way we manage this dichotomy is to maintain relationships which are not too intimate but serve a specific function. When we find ourselves in more intimate relationships, we probably create some distance, by either physically and/or internally withdrawing. Essentially, we feel safer staying on the edges of relationship. Not totally *in* and not totally *out;* we drift somewhere in-between.

Unconsciously we might be waiting, wishing and watching for a time in the future when we can be close to someone and be our full and alive self. We might think, we need to meet the "right" person or get the right amount of recognition, before we can finally feel safe enough to come out of hiding and enter the world.

This dream of revealing our whole self at a future time will remain an unrealised dream, unless we take the risk to do it bit-by-bit now. Indeed, once we have built up a sense of safety and trust with someone, we will need to risk being visible. We will probably hesitate many times before we take this leap of faith however.

Thinking we won't be able to articulate what we need to say, we worry about appearing stupid, babyish or incomprehensible to the other. We might expect the other to reject us, be disinterested, harsh or take advantage of us. And so we remain hesitant and hidden.

Perhaps it is useful to know, we will never feel one hundred percent certain it is okay to come out of hiding; now or in some imagined future. Indeed, the conditions to reveal ourselves will never be perfect. And paradoxically, we will never know if it is okay to reveal our whole aliveness, unless we risk doing it.

So we need to take the risk. It is a calculated risk with at least two conditions however. We must feel *generally* safe with this other person. And we need to be able to sense the *possibility* of being welcomed by them. We may then begin with small risks to test these conditions. Once we know they are "good enough" we can take greater risks of being more fully present and alive in this relationship.

~ ♥ ~

Enjoying Relationships

When we dive into the ocean and our body connects with the
water, there is a moment which takes our breath away.
Is this fear or exhilaration?

Just like our warm body is not used to the temperature of the ocean waters and needs some time to adjust, we might not be familiar with the enjoyment and pleasure found in relationships. Perhaps we are so used to going it alone and being self-sufficient we don't realise this is possible. Or maybe we are more comfortable in relationships which fill a functional need but are devoid of aliveness and joy.

When relationships are *alive*, there is an element of spontaneity and naturalness in them which may feel frightening to us. If as an infant we did not have a safe attachment figure to assist regulate our physiological and emotional states, we may feel scared and overwhelmed by these states in us and others now. No doubt we recognise this regarding what is usually called negative states, such as anger, anxiety or hate. However, we may not realise we also have a similar reaction to positive states, such as excitement, exuberance and love. Perhaps we experience any heightened state of emotion, whether positive or negative, as hazardous and something we need to shut down or avoid.

We might keep a tight lid on our natural desire for enjoyment. In this way we modulate our inner states and keep our self safe. Consciously, we may not even be aware this is something we do. Alternatively, we might allow ourselves pleasure in other aspects of our lives, but keep it controlled in our relationships.

Perhaps we have a habit of avoiding the aspects of relationship which naturally promote aliveness, namely intimacy and pleasure. For example, we might feel unsure when we see delight and welcome in someone else's eyes, so next time we don't look at them or steer clear of them. Maybe we start to get uncomfortable when someone reacts enthusiastically towards us and appears to like us. Although secretly we may like the feeling this gives us, we also feel uneasy about it. Because we would rather forgo pleasure for the certainty of safety, we may move away from these shared moments of human contact.

The intricate world of emotional relationships, even if they are positive, can feel like a minefield for us. Being hesitant about our own aliveness and the aliveness of the other, we avoid jumping into these unknown waters. We stay dry and safe, but at the cost of not feeling the pleasure of swimming and knowing what it's like to be in the ocean.

A bit like diving into the ocean takes our breath away, being fully present with someone can feel really intense for us.

Once we feel safe in a relationship, it is healthy to allow ourselves to experience the pleasure and joy inherent in human contact. Again, we can take this slowly. Gradually becoming accustomed to the various (positive and negative) states of emotional arousal we will experience. Maybe we begin by noticing what it's like to be close with someone: What happens when we share a story with a person who is genuinely interested in what we are saying? What do we feel when we are in contact and looking someone in the eyes?

Since we are new at this, we'll probably feel out of our depth and a bit awkward. Just like it takes time to feel safe with someone, it'll take time to become familiar and comfortable with the aliveness of relationship. We just need a little bit of practice, in staying present in moments of safe and positive connection.

~ ♥ ~

Becoming Embodied

In our journey, we'll need to experience and connect to the sensations and feelings in our body.[p] This can be tricky as some of these are so primitive, deep and painful. It will require great courage and support to allow them to be felt, experienced, held and seen. This is an essential element of our repair. It is when we become grounded in our body that we experience a *real* aliveness, perhaps for the first time in our life.[51]

Whenever we re-orientate to the life in our body, feelings and sensations, we are on path. This includes experiencing all our five senses; touch, smell, sight, hearing and taste. It is good to take our time here; discovering and familiarising ourselves with how our sense perceptions interface with the external world. For example, if we go to the beach. We might notice the sensations of our feet in the sand. Feel the warmth of the sun on our face. Taste and smell the salt and seaweed in the air. Watch and listen as each wave forms and crashes on the shore.

At the same time, we will need to work to reduce the habitual flight into our heads (or intellect). It is healthy for us to re-direct our energy from thinking, ideas, imagination, ungrounded spirituality and other mental constructs, into the present moment experience of our body. Sometimes the breath is a useful conduit to doing this, as is any activity where we use our physical body. For this to be beneficial however, we need to place our attention in our body, rather than in thought.

We probably need to familiarise ourselves with this way of

---

[p] See, Bessel Van der Kolk (2014)

being in our body. Taking our time, we can relax, without worrying we need to do or be something to validate our existence.

As we walk this challenging path of becoming embodied, we slowly begin to experience the pleasure and pain locked in our bodies. Practicing this over time allows the lost parts of our "natural being and aliveness" to become consciously integrated into our physical and emotional sense of self. Here we come home to ourselves and become more fully human.

Our body and the life there-in becomes our home base. It is in this embodiment we begin to feel grounded in a real sense of self.

Becoming Alive

Our survival strategy in the beginning of our life was withdrawal. Today we may continue to withdraw; searching for a place of safety and a way to escape the terror, rage and grief buried in our body.

Perhaps we yearn to be in a womblike surround.[52] This may be accomplished through drug or alcohol use, or a preoccupation with death and re-current thoughts of wanting to die when living becomes too much. Hoping to find a protective shelter and a way to transcend being human, we might be drawn to the world of spirituality. Alternatively, our comfort may reside in the world of ideas, abstraction and intellect, thus keeping away from emotion and connection to the body. We might even continuously seek out intellectual information to understand our internal and external worlds, rather than stepping into experiencing the *reality* of these. In these ways we search for a way to feel safe and to manage the fear, pain and disconnect inside.

There is something here which is essential to understand, but because it is so heart-wrenching, it is an extremely difficult truth to hear. We cannot disconnect or escape from this fear and pain. We must re-connect to it. This means we must *be with* it when it arises; with full awareness and kindness. Not in a drunken or drugged haze, so busy we don't have time for it, wanting to escape it, spiritualise it or intellectualise it.

To experience the pain all over again, to heal, is like adding salt to an open wound. It hurts like hell!

Since this is such a deep and early wound, it needs to be uncovered and managed with the utmost of care and attention. SLOWLY experiencing and being held in the feelings locked and frozen inside of us, will over time allow these states of being to become alive, untangled and incorporated into our growing sense of self.

As already mentioned, we cannot do this alone. Managing these feelings alone at a time when it was impossible for us to do so was the problem. And as Albert Einstein wisely said, we cannot solve a problem with the same solution which created it.

We all require other people to assist us with self-awareness, self-regulation and to witness and be companions on our journey.[53] This is simply part of being human. Everybody requires this, in some shape or form, throughout the life-span. We also need it now, to repair what we missed and assist in the development of our self.[54]

This is a tough and arduous journey. At times it will feel like we are immersed in "fires of hell" and trying to navigate through a "deep dark forest". It might seem like we are drowning and cannot see a way out, experiencing intense periods of hopelessness, to the point of contemplating suicide.

These thoughts and feelings, of hopelessness and death, may be about the pain and difficulties we are currently facing. They could also be a representation of our past, where we learnt it was futile to try and get our needs met from our relational environment, so we gave-up. With support, we may acknowledge this legacy and connect to the extreme pain it carries within us.

It is possible we will feel uncertain about reaching out for help during these times. If we can build the courage to take this risk however, we have the possibility of getting the support we need. If this feels too much for us, perhaps we can go to a place where there are other people, for example, a café, the beach or the library. In this way, we can *just be with* others around us and not feel so alone. Sometimes though, the only thing we are capable of at these times is taking one breath after another. Breathing in...I am alive. Breathing out...I can just be here. It can be a relief to know there is nothing more we need to do. We can just be here, breathing in and breathing out. Although in infancy our only option was to give-up, now we are an adult, when we feel bereft or hopeless, we can remember that we have other options available to us.

~ ♥ ~

Crossing the Chasm

Since in our early experience our painful feelings felt dangerous and overwhelming, to re-experience these as an adult will initially seem just as dangerous and overwhelming. It is important we choose someone to assist us with this. Someone wiser who understands where these feelings are coming from. And strong enough to stay with us in these feelings, without being overwhelmed or needing to withdraw themselves. With support we can slowly begin to feel again, without needing to go away. Over time, we will understand these feelings are not as dangerous or overwhelming as they were in infancy.

In the beginning of our life, our painful feelings didn't have thought or meaning attached to them, as our brain wasn't fully developed in these higher processes. Today when we re-experience these feelings, which were rendered to our bodily unconscious as an infant, we do have thought. Hence, our mind can go a "little wild" in trying to make sense and explain what these emotional states now mean.

This is dangerous territory to enter. If we entertain these types of thoughts, we may feel as if we are going mad.

If this occurs, and no doubt it probably will if this is our legacy, we need to over time, tame these thoughts. And *be with* the physical feeling only. This is what we missed when we were most vulnerable as an infant, someone to stay with us and hold us while we experienced these emotions. And so, this is what we are required to do now.

No doubt, this is a precarious bridge to cross. Simply *being with* and connecting to our physical feelings, while taming the thoughts of our mind; will take us, one step at a time, across to the other side. Without this finely tuned balance, we will get lost, think we are going crazy, feel afraid, want to die and experience total over-whelm. Indeed, if we experience these painful states and allow our mind to continue the story of our past, (e.g. it is dangerous, we will die, there is no-one there for us, we are totally alone, we will not survive, it is too much) we will experience it as such.

While "being with" the pain, we do not engage our thinking mind in the story of our past. In this way the energy of emotion becomes embodied, disperses and transforms.

We may utilise our thinking mind in a way which is beneficial for this crossing. One way we can do this is to consider how this emotional part of us, in so much pain, would like us to respond to it. Perhaps we bring a picture to our mind of what it looks like. We might even imagine sitting with it for a while, bringing some gentle attention to it, asking what it needs from us right now and listening for its response. Of course, this is tricky to do when another part of us just wants to shut it down, have it stop, cut it off and get rid of it.

We can experiment a little here, imagining different ways to re-spond to our pain and then trying them out. Investigating for our-selves what the outcome of these different ways of *being with* our pain is like. For example, what happens when we shut it down, compared to when we listen and be gentle with it. Through this type of self-enquiry, we will discover the methods which work for us and the methods which don't.

If we can allow these intense feelings to "play out" and become embodied, we will come through to the other side and have an experiential understanding *we survived*; we got through it and are okay. Since however, this was not the experience at the beginning of our life, we usually avoid any reminder or inkling of such. This includes feelings of terror or being overwhelmed and thoughts of annihilation or going mad. To cross this chasm however, we will eventually need to face these.

During this crossing, we will need to use every ounce of our warrior and warrioress like strength to *be with* the terror and overwhelm. We will need to hold strong and know these thoughts of annihilation and madness are not a true indication of our full mental state or reality. Most importantly, we will need the support of someone we trust, to hold a protected space for these feelings and a belief in our sanity.

At the most difficult points of the crossing, it will be useful to remember, in some part of our being, we are an adult now and therefore not as vulnerable as when we were fully dependent on another for our survival. Hence, the experience of precariousness in our current situation is actually not like it was in the beginning of our life, even though it is felt as if it were. It is prudent to understand the difference here. We are remembering the experience of our past, but in the present are not in the same life and death situation.

There will be times on this journey when we feel like we are stepping into the unknown; like navigating the dark without a torch. During these periods we might expect all sorts of "ghosts" to jump out at us. It is best at these times to stay firmly grounded. Breathing...I am in my body. Feeling my feet on the ground...the earth holds me.

It may feel comforting at these times to know we can depend on some certainty. For example, we can be sure the earth will hold us. We can also be certain the sun will rise at dawn and then go down at dusk.

Keeping connected to our safe person is also useful, even if it is through our imagination. For example, we keep in mind the feeling of safety and comfort we have when with them. We might even imagine them walking beside us in this unknown terrain.

Finally, if at times we become disorientated, we may re-orientate our focus to something we have discovered is enjoyable, grounding and soothing. For example: Going for a walk on the beach or in the forest. Being in water (e.g. having a shower/bath or going for a swim). Talking and connecting with someone. Being warmly hugged by someone we feel safe with. Breathing, playing music, being creative, journaling, gardening, being in nature and being with animals.

~ ♥ ~

Creative Potential

Due to a thinner than average filter over our unconscious, we are probably less defended against the deeper and darker aspects of our human nature.[55] This is both a positive and negative experience for us.

Access to the depths of our human psyche gives us a richness, others do not necessarily have, thus enabling true creativity.[56] However, this deep inner world may also feel overwhelmingly destructive and hence be difficult to navigate.

With time, containment and maturity, we can form a healthier relationship with our unconscious and the energies of creation and destruction inherent in our "being and aliveness". In this way we utilise its potential, allowing it to be a source of deep understanding, innovative ideas and creativity.

This potential will only be realised if grounded and made manifest on earth. One of the dangers of this position is that the *gifts* are unrealised and remain as an untapped resource.

This occurs when we keep our *aliveness* locked in an inner sanctum; not daring to make ourselves visible. When we don't relate to others or the external environment with our fullness, we stunt our experience of life. In this way we only live an imagined life, forever dreaming about the vast possibilities in the future. If however, we are able to work at being present, visible and embodied on this earth, our creative potential can become grounded and real.

Our potential may also remain unrealised because we are unable to harness and utilise the energies of destruction and creation. We might be so focused on survival and avoiding the terror of annihilation (i.e. destruction), we have no energy left to thrive and truly live (i.e. create). Here we are so entwined in struggles of life and death, sanity and madness, existence and annihilation; it is impossible to direct our energy for creative purposes. When we find ourselves here, we need to work at containment. This includes all we have spoken about thus far (i.e. safety, connection and embodiment). It also includes building a stronger sense of self, so we can contain the intensity of "being and aliveness" which flows through us, rather than be overwhelmed by it. In this way we strengthen our ability to embody and contain the energies of destruction, so we may then utilise the energies of creation.

Finally, to realise our creative potential, we also need to connect to and understand the emotional pain we've kept locked away. Once we consciously welcome and make room for all the emotional parts of our self, the destructive impact of unacknowledged emotions will diminish.

~ ♥ ~

Our Needs

Since our experience occurred so early, it is important we understand and are realistic about our sensitivities and needs. Here we provide ourselves with the space, nourishment, care and attention we require.

We may experience acute sensitivity; within our self, towards others and in our environment.

More than most people, we need to make room in our life for our sensitivity to safety. Paying attention to when and with whom we feel safe and unsafe. Then re-orientating ourselves towards people and environments in which we feel safe and away from those we don't. We also need to be clear about what our safety needs are and be proactive in taking care of them, even if it seems "silly" or atypical to the norm. For example, if we go to a social event, we might need the option to leave if we become overwhelmed. Rather than an avoidance strategy, this is a safety requirement, so we feel okay to participate more fully in life.

We are probably sensitive to anyone *really* seeing us. Experiencing this as somewhat risky, we may gravitate to people and situations where we can hide or withdraw, including those who tend to be harsh, cold, insensitive or preoccupied with themselves. We will need to become more conscious about this, taking risks to show ourselves with people who are interested in us and with whom we feel safe.

Our relational needs may seem contradictory. We might get tired and drained around people, but find it difficult to be completely alone. We will need to find a balance between, being alone (and re-charging) and being connected in relationship. Although this applies to most people, it is essential we get the balance which is right for us.[57]

Finally, we may experience sensitivities in our environment. Loud noises, people arguing, bright lights and crowds, may feel overstimulating for us. Consequently, we may need to arrange our environment, particularly our home and work, so we feel a sense of calm and safety. We will probably also need to spend time in nature and with animals, to re-calibrate our energy systems.

Our sensitivity is both a gift and a burden.
We will need to understand it, bring it into
balance and utilise it, so it is a constructive
rather than a destructive force.

Our sensitivity is part of who we are. We might think we need to get rid of it, so we can stop getting hurt or can fit better into this (seemingly insensitive) world. This is not true! We need to make use of our exquisite ability to deeply feel and be attuned to the subtle. In this way we bring the gift of sensitivity into the world.

To do this however, we need our sensitivity to be rooted in a place of strength. Meaning, we need to become embodied, building a stronger sense of self. This will allow us to be open, not afraid anymore of participating in this world and showing our whole self. In this way our sensitivity becomes a strength and resource we can draw upon.

Like a house, we build a stronger sense of self from the ground up. This means, we connect with our "natural being and aliveness" and allow our self to emerge from here. Much of this work, for us, will involve the physical and emotional domains, as this is perhaps where our limitations lie. While our mental and spiritual domains, where we may experience greater strength, are resources we can draw upon.

Physically, we may need to ground ourselves and connect to the life in our body. We may also have physical sensitivities we need to take care of. For example; a delicate nervous system, poor immune functioning, tightness in our muscles and ligaments, difficulty with digestion, weakness in our lower back, fatigue. Taking extra care with our daily physical needs, such as eating well, resting and exercising, will also be beneficial for us.

Emotionally, we probably need to learn how to identify a larger range of feelings and then practice expressing them with people we feel safe with. Finding ways to contain our feelings so they don't overwhelm us, will also be necessary. Finally, we would benefit from finding avenues where we can experience and express our rich inner world.

It is possible we are stronger in the mental and spiritual domains. For example: we may be attuned to the subtle; understand the unseen and immaterial world; have easier access to the spiritual and symbolic dimensions; perceive the energy inherent in all living things; have a unique aliveness, realness and authenticity; be curious and want to understand how things work; be able to see connections others do not see; have a vivid imagination; be truly creative. These are resources we have, which we can utilise and draw upon to assist us on this journey.

Because we need to tackle our repair from the ground up, we will probably engage in more than one avenue to heal. Some of the modalities we might find therapeutic, include; psychological therapy, meditation, body work (e.g. massage therapies, cranial-sacral therapy), energy healing (e.g. reiki, kinesiology), physical movement (e.g. sports or exercise we enjoy, building core strength, weight training, dancing), meditative movement (e.g. yoga, tai-chi, chi-going), creativity (e.g. writing, art, craft, woodwork, dance, music, drama), meeting with interest or healing groups, being in nature and finding personal relationships which are supportive and nourishing.

In choosing what we need at any given time, we may listen to our heart and soul, allowing it to guide us. The *person* conducting the therapy will be an important factor in our repair. This again re-iterates the importance of relationship. It may be prudent then to seek out people and groups where we feel safe, held in mind and supported, and to remember we do not need to continue if this is not the case.

~ ♥ ~

Navigating this Path

Those of us who do this work and cross this chasm, have a deep sense of *knowing* inside of us; if we want to live a full human life, we have little choice but to take each step along this journey. There is often a life or death forced-choice feel to it. We want to be whole and fully alive, rather than continue to exist in a robot-like way, but somewhere deep inside we are in touch with the precariousness of this path. So we often take each step with a sense of trepidation.

This repair takes time. It may even take our whole lifetime. When we think about it like this, we can breathe easy and say to ourselves, "There is time...I do not have to rush...I can be patient and gentle with myself...I can take it slow...There is space for all of me here".

In the beginning of our life we were shocked into hiding, so now we cannot be shocked out of it.

To get the benefits of this long journey, we need to stay the course. In our darkest hours then, we may need something bigger than our (individual) self to continue. This motivation may vary amongst us. Perhaps we want a healthy intimate relationship, have children we want to parent well, are a therapist and want to assist people who have been through similar experiences. Maybe our reason is more philosophical or spiritual. The specific motive does not matter, as long as it holds some greater meaning for us to use as inspiration through our most difficult times.

It is up to us individually, to decide how far we are willing to go. Our wise or intuitive mind will know when we get to a certain point, whether it is enough and we are satisfied knowing this is what we can live with, or whether it feels like we have little choice but to continue. If we stop, we can always re-engage with the process at a later point in time. If we continue, we can always take some rest breaks. There are no set rules here. It is something we must each decide for ourselves.

This is our individual path and journey, so it is up to each of us to decide how we navigate it. We may seek advice from people we trust and from those with knowledge in this area, but we will need to make the final decisions. Each of us is *responsible* for our self and will be the one to reap the rewards of the internal work we do.

My deepest hope for us who have this legacy, is that we take one step at a time towards becoming visible; allowing our full *being* and *aliveness* to be seen. This is the essential part of us which has been hiding deeply inside for so long, waiting for the right opportunity to come out, be reborn and to show its face. Although scared and sensitive, this part yearns to be fully alive. It too wants to take part and dance its rhythm on this earth.

This dance may be different to what we have been doing up to now. It may also be different to what is expected of us. But it is who we are; our true dance. If we allow it, our heart and soul will guide us in taking each step on this path, even though at times this will feel unfamiliar and perhaps even terrifying.

This is not an easy path we have found ourselves on. Reaching out and getting relational support, so we can grow, will be essential. We require the wisdom, strength and guidance of at least one other person, who can listen well, hold us in mind, stay with us when things get tough and keep the hope for us when we are unable to do it for ourselves.

Phase Two

A solid and secure foundation

(3-6 months to 15 months)

In our metaphor of building a house, this second phase is analogous to laying the concrete foundation. The foundation must be
secure and provide a stable enough base for the house to be built
upon it. If the foundation is not secure or stable enough, the structure of the house will inevitably be compromised.

Nourishment of Needs

I can depend upon you

My needs are okay | I am supported | I have enough |
I am satisfied

Once we have determined the land is safe and secure enough to hold our developing house, we are ready to lay the foundation. If the land is unstable, the foundation will be compromised, unless someone detects the trouble in time and reinforces it in some way.

This is the same for the developing infant. If the initial relational environment is not able to provide a safe attachment for the newborn, it is quite likely this next phase, which concerns the dependency needs of the baby, may also be impaired.

However, there are instances, where a major stressor may occur in the parents' life around the time of birth, but once passed, the capacity to care for the needs of their baby becomes favourable. These stressors may relate to the pregnancy, birth and first few months of the newborn's life. For example, a problematic birth, a premature birth or medical condition where the infant needs to stay in hospital. Alternatively, the stressor may relate to external circumstances which just so happen to coincide with the birth of the baby. For example, death of a significant person in the parents' life, sudden work stress such as a redundancy or a sudden major physical/medical illness of someone in the family. These types of stressors are not necessarily embedded in the fabric of the family environment, but may occur for caregivers who would usually be considered "good enough". In these types of situations, when the stressor is reduced or resolved, the relational environment then becomes "good enough" again.

On the other hand, the prognosis may be quite different if the infant is born into a relational environment with a set point which is "not good enough". In these situations, the environment is not lacking due to a recent stressor or something unusual occurring, but rather as a pre-existing condition. Since this is the general tone or atmosphere the infant is born into, the possibility of it suddenly becoming more conducive when the baby is three or six months old is unrealistic.

In a more encouraging scenario however, there may be a situation where the caregiver(s) receives some intervention or assistance which improves their ability to parent. Early intervention may have a positive influence on the relational environment and allow the parent(s) to form a secure attachment to their growing infant.[58] This can mitigate the negative impact on the developing baby.

In other situations, the environmental failure may begin in phase two. It is possible the newborn has been able to form a safe and secure attachment relationship during their first three or six months, but then experiences problems in the relational environment after this time. Again, uncontrollable stress factors may be a reason for a change in the relational environment during this second phase. For example, the main attachment figure is diagnosed with a serious illness at this time and finds the increasing demands of their own needs, coupled with an increase in the demand of their infant's needs, very difficult to navigate. This would be worsened if there was little or no extra support for the attachment figure during this time. Another way this change can occur, is if the attachment figure is "good enough" with providing a safe and secure relational environment when the baby is still relatively passive, in the few months post birth. But finds it difficult and more challenging when their baby becomes more *lively*, energetic and curious.

Newborns certainly have a rich internal world and engage in relationship. However, it is from about three months of age when this becomes increasingly apparent to the outside observer.[59] The infant's ability to *communicate*, their internal world to the external world, grows exponentially during this second phase. For example, an infant's physical ability goes through a considerable developmental leap, from small movements to walking confidently. Alongside this, a wider range of emotional states, such as anger, frustration, fear, anxiety, sadness, shock, surprise, joy, happiness and contentment are more observable. Consequently, this can be a more challenging phase for some parents. Their developing baby, rather than sleeping most of the day, becomes more lively, responsive, demanding and with a growing ability to express themselves.

Along the same lines, if a caregiver has idealised the experience of having a baby, during this phase they may struggle coming to terms with the reality. For example, if someone has only contemplated the positive aspects of being a parent, such as the stereotypical nurturing mother figure who serenely breastfeeds her newborn. This type of image is more easily matched in the first few months of the newborn's life. However, as a baby becomes *alive* with all their dependent needs, the real breadth of the parenting task becomes apparent. This reality may confront the image one holds of the task of parenting, and/or challenge the image one holds of oneself as a parent.

In some instances, the caregivers will be able to learn from this challenge and change their understanding of what their role of parenting requires, integrating a more balanced and realistic view. In other instances, the caregivers may not like the face of reality and find the confrontation to their idealised view too difficult to navigate. They may then deal with this challenge in a way which allows them to keep their idealised image intact. For example, blame the baby for being "too demanding" and become angry at their dependent needs. Alternatively, they might think their baby isn't enough of something (e.g. not cute enough, doesn't smile on demand), so they try and shape the infant to meet their own needs and expectations. This caregiver may also engage in the aspects of parenting corresponding to their ideal, while negating the parts that don't. Such approaches, where the infant is deemed "too much" or "not enough", are likely to result in disconnection from the baby's true needs.

T his second phase of development is an important time, where the baby learns they can (or cannot) depend upon another person to meet their needs. This is a long time period in "baby world" and the needs of the infant during this time do evolve. Perhaps it is useful then to divide this phase into two approximate periods, before the baby crawls (3 to 9 months) and after the baby crawls and begins walking (9 to 15 months). For ease, let's call these periods pre-crawling and post-crawling.

Throughout the pre-crawling stage an infant is extremely dependent upon their caregiver to meet all their needs, including the ability to regulate their physiological and emotional states. In contrast to a newly born, who has quite limited ways to communicate their needs (e.g. crying), during this phase a baby's ability to physically communicate their needs gradually increases. From three months of age, they slowly begin to move their physical body more. This means, in addition to vocalising, they can communicate physically, by perhaps flailing around, arching their back, kicking their legs and moving their arms; enabling greater expression and aliveness in their communication. From about six months of age this communicative ability expands again, incrementally moving their whole body; rolling over, rocking while on hands and knees, sitting up, sliding on the floor and then eventually crawling.

Crawling heralds a significant developmental progression. From here they gradually stand on their legs with assistance, stand on their own, practice walking and then eventually walk with confidence. This substantial increase in physical movement allows them to explore the world on their own. This post-crawling stage also heralds the gradual start of verbal language. Basic one-word communications, coupled with the increase in physical ability, allows the infant an expanded repertoire to communicate if they are distressed, satisfied, wanting connection or wanting to explore.

The post-crawling stage is also the time when the baby begins to experience increasing separation from their attachment figure. Consequently, it is exemplified by contrasting experiences. The baby can now move towards objects in the outside world on their own, increasing exploration and play. However, the realisation they are separate from their attachment figure brings anxiety. This dynamic creates a complex mix of needs for the caregiver to navigate. The baby is now more able to communicate the *rhythm* of their needs, by moving toward and away from their attachment figure and other objects. But will require reassurance and emotional support to negotiate the increase in separation-anxiety.

As can be seen, this second foundational phase is an important developmental time, centred on the evolving needs of the infant. It therefore requires the parent to stay attuned and responsive to the complex and changing needs of their baby. This includes; maintaining a secure base for safety and connection, as well as assistance with regulating emotional and physiological states. Then as the infant begins to crawl, holding a space for exploration and navigation of increasing separation also becomes important.

"THE ESSENTIAL TASK OF THE FIRST YEAR OF HUMAN LIFE IS NOW SEEN AS THE CREATION OF A SECURE ATTACHMENT BOND OF EMOTIONAL COMMUNICATION BETWEEN THE INFANT AND THE PRIMARY CAREGIVER."
Allan N. Shore, (2012). *The Science of the Art of Psychotherapy.*

When it Becomes Tricky

If caregivers have had insufficient parenting themselves at this stage, without further intervention, they might find it difficult to attune and respond to the increasing complexity of their infant's needs. If as a parent, one's own childhood needs were not seen or judged negatively (e.g. too much of something or not enough of something) and hence not responded to in an attuned way, it might be tricky to know how to be attuned to these same needs in another.

Since this stage is about nourishment of needs (i.e. being supported in both dependency and growing exploration), a parent's own conflict about this will influence the way they respond to their infant. Indeed, if we are uncomfortable with certain dependent needs of our own (e.g. needing emotional or physical support), we will probably find it hard to be attuned and respond to these needs in another. If we are then a parent, this same dynamic may occur in regard to our infant's needs for (emotional or physical) support. Alternatively, if we are very comfortable with dependency and receiving support from others, but fear our own independence and aloneness, we may have difficulty when someone wants some separation and space from us. If then we are a parent, we may become anxious when our infant begins exploring, being more self-determining and separating from us.

In a similar vein, sometimes unhelpful ideas about parenting are passed consciously and unconsciously down the generational lines. Some examples of these include: thinking it's best to limit holding a baby, so they don't get "spoilt" or too familiar with being held; allowing an infant to cry themselves out so they learn to self-soothe; providing lots of non-human interaction in the environment for stimulation of growth; and restricting exploration due to anxiety and fear of something negative happening.

The influence of modernity also needs be considered in the way one parents, particularly at this important phase of development. Sometimes caregivers are simply too busy with other demands on their time to respond in an attuned way to their infant. Our culture, in its own unintegrated split, encourages *doing*, busyness and working; rather than *being*, connecting and playing. For example, rather than *being with* feelings, we tend to want to *do something* to fix or stop the feeling, so we can then get on with what we consider as more important. For healthy psychological growth however, infants require us to *Be, Connect and Play*.

Repair in Attachment

It is important to note, breaches in the attachment relationship will occur with all parent and infant dyads. Parents are humans, dealing with their own internal and external demands, thus variously affecting their ability to be attuned and respond to their infant. An essential difference in the secure attachment style, compared to the insecure and (particularly) the disorganised styles, is the repair provided by the parent to re-establish the attachment relationship, after a breach.

Repair is crucial. It is not necessarily the breach in attachment which causes the insecurity or disorganisation. It is the lack of repair to re-establish the attuned and responsive attachment, which causes the problem.[60]For example, let's imagine a parent who during dinner finds themselves angry at their nine-month-old baby who is tired, a bit grizzly, not eating, squelching food between their fingers and rubbing it in their hair. Let's say the parent is also tired and feels stressed about a problem they are personally dealing with. Feeling suddenly very irritated by their baby's behaviour, they grab and restrain their infant's hands, lean forward and angrily say, "Stop it". The infant responds by crying and becoming distressed. In repair of this breach, the parent firstly realises the attachment relationship has been ruptured and that their infant needs help to feel better. They then tune into themselves and their infant; internally soothing their own anger and allowing themselves to empathically feel their infant's distress. Finally, with a more soothing facial expression, voice intonation and physical touch, the parent can take care of their infant's distress, and thus re-establish the attachment relationship.

As we can see, repair is an active internal and external process. Firstly, there needs to be awareness a rupture in the relationship has occurred, followed by an understanding it needs to be repaired. Secondly, the caregiver needs to self-regulate their own emotional state and tune into their infant's state. When the caregiver soothes their own emotional state, the baby is also able to regulate their emotions through a limbic resonance with their parent's state. When the caregiver feels calmer, they can respond more effectively to their infant's distress. Furthermore, when the caregiver empathetically tunes into their infant's distress, the baby through limbic resonance senses they are emotionally held by their attachment figure, which also acts to reassure and soothe them. Thirdly, the caregiver works to change their previous behaviour. Turning towards their baby, they attune physically, emotionally and mentally to what is needed, respond accordingly and hence re-establish the secure attachment.

However, if no repair takes place, the situation looks quite different. Let's follow this example where the baby is now crying because of the parent's breach. Without recognition by the caregiver, he/she may act in a way which increases the baby's distress and emotional dysregulation. For example, perhaps the caregiver increases their angry response (e.g. yells louder, physically restrains their infant, force feeds them). Maybe the caregiver pleads with their infant to stop crying or starts crying themselves. Perhaps they ignore the distress by distracting their baby (e.g. jollying them into being happy, putting an iPad with an animation in front of them). They may also emotionally disengage (e.g. just sit looking at their infant waiting for them to calm down). Finally, perhaps they actively disengage both physically and emotionally (e.g. take the food away and leave their infant crying in the highchair, leave the room and do not return until their infant stops crying).

In all these non-repair situations, the baby is left to deal with the initial rupture and consequent ruptures on their own. This becomes an extremely distressing situation for the infant as they are *literally* unable to regulate themselves and require the attachment relationship to assist them. Adding a further layer of distress, the infant, already dysregulated due to the initial breach in attachment, becomes even more distressed at the increasing misattunement of the caregiver. At a certain point, this distress and dysregulation, without repair and assistance from the caregiver, is untenable for the infant to continue to experience.[61]

If the natural resources of the infant (e.g. crying, frustration, anger, distress) to get their needs met, do not elicit an attuned response from their relational environment, they have no other choice at this stage but to negate their needs. Before this point is reached however, the baby will show they have a need, for example by crying. If a need isn't met, (e.g. not held or connected to, not comforted when distressed, goes hungry, or if the care is done in an anxious, angry or disengaged manner) the baby will initially protest this failure by showing signs of frustration and anger. If this protest again is not met, the baby will become highly distressed. When this again is not responded to, they will eventually fall into a sense of despair and hopelessness. If this type of interaction continually repeats itself, the baby implicitly learns that no matter what they do their relational environment is unresponsive; so they give-up.

To survive, the infant needs to then organise their psychological experience around the failure of their relational environment. The part of their "being and aliveness" not met (e.g. need to be assisted with their distress) is negated or suppressed. Furthermore, the infant will learn to adapt and comply with this failure in their environment.

When what is inherently natural is not responded to, the implicit message is there is something wrong or bad about that instinct, desire or need. Since the baby is completely dependent on their caregivers for survival and does not have the brain mechanisms (e.g. neocortex) to make sense of their world, they are unable to consider the reality of their situation. That is, understand their needs are natural and normal, and that the problem lies in the failure of their relational environment, rather than in them.

The part, of the infant's "being and aliveness", which is negated or suppressed doesn't just disappear. It remains unintegrated in the bodily unconscious and consequently is not available to proceed through further development.[62] In essence, the need remains alive in an unconscious way. For example, if a baby cuts off their need for a responsive caregiver and consequently complies by stopping crying, they will appear as if they don't need somebody to assist regulate their distress. However, embodied in the unconscious, this baby continues to cry; grief stricken, hopeless, but still needing what they didn't get. Thus, whilst this infant may appear "easy" and "not need much", to a perceptive observer, they will have a disconnected, melancholy and depleted feel to them.

If this environmental failure continues, in phase three and onwards, the infant may begin to reverse the roles of caretaking. That is, they become a pseudo-caretaker for the needs of their parent. In this way, they can survive by denying the reality of their relational environment. This strategy enables the deprivation not to be felt, rage at unmet needs to be kept under lock and key, as well as a sense of control over a frightening reality. This situation may particularly occur, when the infant has a natural tendency towards being sensitive to the needs of others, the family culture encourages such caretaking, or the parent unconsciously requires this due to their own unmet needs.

The Legacy

If an infant at this phase generally experiences their caregivers as dependable and attuned to their needs, they will understand relationships (and the world) as a place of support, care and satisfaction. This foundation is a strong basis for the whole self to develop.

If this has been our experience, we will know within relationship we are able to get our needs for nourishment, support, love and connection met. We will be able to depend on others, implicitly understanding it is okay to ask for what we need and be able to take in and receive what is given.[63] We are also okay with another depending upon us and providing for some of their needs. To be in relationship feels good and mutually satisfying. There may of course be varying degrees to which we experience this, but our general foundation is secure, rather than the alternative.

If an infant's experience is such that they cannot reliably depend on their caregivers to meet their needs, relationships are felt to be depriving, lacking care, unsupportive and dissatisfying. If the deprivation of need is severe, dependency in relationships will be experienced as painful and dangerous. The infant feels rage at their unmet needs and embodies a sense of longing and hunger for natural needs not satisfied. They must of course continue to grow, but now it is in a depleted way.

If this has been our legacy, we may experience much angst around the satisfaction of our needs, particularly within our relationships. We have implicitly embodied a difficult dynamic in relation to the specific needs (X) which were unmet. The formula of this dynamic goes a little like this: I naturally need X, but I have learnt not to need X. Unconsciously, I long for and seek satisfaction of X, but believe X cannot be satisfied. The way this plays out in our life may occur in one or more of the following three ways:

(a) I feel an insatiable need for X (e.g. I am always hungry to be cared for and loved; depleted) and so I grab onto any source, without discernment, where I think it might be satisfied. However, I remain unsatisfied and thus depleted. Because I either cling to sources which are not truly satisfying, or cannot take-in and be satisfied by "good enough" sources.

(b) Whenever I start to feel the need for X, I dismiss or cut this need off. So rather than seeking fulfillment of this natural need, I convince myself I do not need it and push on without it. Even though I do not always consciously feel the need for X (e.g. to be cared for and loved) I am still depleted. Again, if X happens to be available, I simply dismiss it without taking it in, soldier on without satisfaction and continue to be depleted.

(c) I think I do not need X, but am very perceptive seeing others that need X, and so I provide it for them. I am somewhat compulsive in my giving of X, as I must give X to keep my own feelings of deprivation of X out of awareness. My giving of X may have unconscious "strings attached" as I give X as a way for me to satisfy my own need of X. Even when X happens to be available for me, I will sacrifice my own satisfaction to give it to someone else. Finally, my giving of X eventually becomes laced with unconscious rage and anger, because my need of X remains unsatisfied and I continue to be depleted.

What this Means for Us...Now

If our early experience of relationship was one where our needs were not cared for in a "good enough" way, as adults the connection to our own needs (and the needs of others) is probably fraught with difficulty. Cycling between extremes of over-identifying and under-identifying with our needs, we are unable to find a healthy balance. We may also have trouble taking in or asking for support and perhaps feel dissatisfied within our relationships.

Our road to repair requires us to get in touch with the grieving, enraged and deprived infant inside of us. Uncovering the grief and hopelessness of our natural needs not provided for, we begin to know and mourn the profound loss we experienced. Embodying the rage of the infant who expected to be cared for, we gain a sense of strength and begin to understand it is okay to have needs. Finally, we are required to touch the pain of deprivation buried deeply inside us. It is here we become less afraid of our needs and now as an adult take responsibility for nourishing the child within.

Over and Under Identification of Needs

If as an infant our experience in this second foundational phase was "not good enough" and there has been no opportunity for repair, we will as adults have difficulty with our natural needs. At a very basic and physical level we may not be in tune with our *hunger*. Indeed, we may either over-identify with our needs (for example, we are unable to tolerate any form of emptiness or hunger), or we may under-identify with our needs and not feel the natural desire for nourishment and satiation. To carry this example further, the over-identification of this hunger need may lead to overeating or never going without, while the under-identification results in a controlled restraint. This situation also occurs with our other needs, such as desires to be cared about and supported within our relationships.

If we over-identify with this need, we cannot tolerate being alone and so constantly seek to be filled and cared about by somebody else. We fear being alone as it reminds us of the distress and deprivation of relationship we experienced as an infant, and so we cling to someone else to try and avoid this pain. In this case, we may remain in relationships which are not healthy and not particularly nourishing, unconsciously replaying this childhood wound, while all the while trying to avoid it. Perhaps we are overly accommodating to the other person because we are afraid to ask for our needs, create conflict, or see the reality of the relationship.

We are probably not direct or assertive in asking for and getting our desires satisfied. The infant inside of us however, still angry at not having rightful needs met, covertly expects the other person to meet our requirements. This is where it becomes complicated for us, as although we unconsciously feel entitled to our desires being met, consciously we are not connected to what our real needs are. We may feel shame about our feelings of *need* and *greed*, and so find it extremely difficult to be direct in asking for their satisfaction. It is also possible we believe the other person should know exactly what we want without us having to ask for it. Since we often have an uncanny ability to know what the other person wants, we find it difficult to understand how they don't "just know" what we need too. Since people cannot read our mind, we are often disappointed in our relationships and perhaps think they do not care about us. Unconsciously however, we may feel unworthy of being cared about.

We may have times when we collapse into a state of helplessness, feeling there is *nothing I can do* and there is *nothing you can do*. Here we may become stuck in a state of depression. This feeling of depression not only mimics how we felt as an infant, but like then, serves a protective function. Depression protects us from feeling the real grief, rage and deprivation locked inside of us. These feelings are raw, intense and bring us back to a time in our life where our dependency on another could have felt endangering.

Sometimes we feel so consumed by our need we cannot bear for it to remain unfulfilled. Not filling the need as soon as possible may feel like impending danger to us. For example, we may never be without food as we feel anxious when we start to feel hungry or do not have access to food. Similarly, we may be pre-occupied with our relationships, fear being alone and so we always make sure we are in a relationship.

In this position we may also have issues with addictions, particularly to sources which can supply us with a dependent supply of satisfaction and thereby act as a substitute attachment figure. Food is obviously a good choice here as it is easily accessible, and we can have control over when, what and how much we eat. In this way, food becomes a reliable source of satisfaction and thus attachment. Alcohol, tobacco, prescription drugs and other drugs may also work in this way. Addictions to sex, pornography and work are other examples of surrogate attachment figures, where we try and get our needs met. With these addictions we are often trying to get what we never got as an infant and child; a reliable source of connection, nourishment and fulfilment.

Basically, our unconscious drive here is to never be without and to have control over satisfaction of our needs. We don't want to re-experience the deprivation and powerlessness we felt as an infant.

However, using surrogate attachment sources is fraught with difficulty. Underneath this *never going without*, we may have feelings of self-loathing and disgust about how we are fulfilling our need. We can also end up feeling *out of control* as we cycle between our needs being satisfied (when we have our supply) and needs going unmet (when we don't have our supply). Furthermore, if we look closely enough, we realise we are not truly satisfied or fulfilled by these sources.

These addictive attachments, although seemingly providing for us, begin to work in our disfavour, resulting in exactly what we got as an infant; disconnection, hunger and deprivation. With any addiction we are usually disconnected from ourselves and often from other people. Although on the surface it appears to feed us, in fact it is not the nourishment we are deeply wanting and so we remain hungry. Consequently, we are caught in a cycle of deprivation of our needs, exactly as we experienced as an infant, except this time we are doing it to ourselves. Indeed, we are not pursuing our true needs of connection, nourishment and fulfilment. And so the infant within continues to grieve and rage at real needs unmet.

Alternatively, if we under-identify with our needs, we will minimise or disown our needs, particularly for care and support in relationship. If we had to negate our need for connection, we may not seek out or experience relationships for their ability to comfort, support and provide us with true intimacy. In this way we avoid our feelings of grief, rage and deprivation, by convincing ourselves we do not need. Some of us may still be in touch with some of our longings for care and support. However, we believe this desire won't be met and so we unconsciously sabotage the possibility of this need being satisfied. For example, we may not bother to seek it out, not take a risk to gratify it, give-up prematurely or act in ways (e.g. aggressively, dismissingly) which obstructs someone giving to us.

In this self-reliant position, we do not take the risk of depending upon another person. We still hold the grief and rage of having to grow up without the assistance of someone, but we deal with it in a *just got to keep soldiering on* sort of attitude. Hence, rather than collapsing into helplessness we push on, even though we are deprived and depleted with little internal resources.

We may have times where we overestimate what we can accomplish, pushing ourselves and ignoring our needs, until we are exhausted. For example, we may work long hours, taking care of the needs of others. Since we are increasingly depleting ourselves however, there will be a time in the future when we will collapse. Often if we relate to this under-identification of needs, we will collapse in a way which is not in our conscious control, such as becoming physically ill. In this way we get the rest we need from overextending ourselves, but still do not consciously connect to our needs.

Often in this position we may have a knack for seeing and responding to the needs of other people. Again, this allows us to deny our own neediness. Rather than feeling devoured by our own hunger, we externalise this and feel devoured by the hunger of others. Hence, there may be tension in our "helping" as unconsciously we are angry at providing for another, while going hungry ourselves. In addition, since we are giving from a position of depletion, we feel even more depleted from giving and as a result eventually may feel aggrieved and resentful.

We are like a soldier who is tired and worn from the battle of fighting to survive without assistance. We feel angry at having to keep on going without help. But since we believe there is no other way, we trudge through each day, perhaps secretly longing for someone to magically see our wishes and help us.

Regarding this over and under identification of need, we probably seem to do more of one than the other, although both will operate within us. We may identify with one more consciously, but the other is waiting in the background. For example, we may be in touch with our sense of collapse and helplessness, until we get an inkling the other person is getting tired of our demands and so we suddenly show them we do not have any requirements; everything is okay and our demands disappear. Perhaps we even become quite proactive, and with a burst of energy line up our next relationship where we hope our desires will finally be satisfied. Alternatively, if we tend towards under-identifying with our needs, we may cycle through periods of over-extending ourselves, often helping others, while being self-reliant ourselves. We may begin this cycle with a lot of energy, but then slowly start trudging through our days, until suddenly it is too much, and we collapse into exhaustion.

Our needs are fuelled with angst.

Unmet Needs

Of course, no infant, has had the experience of all their needs being attuned and responded to exactly as they require. However, a perfect response always, is not necessarily conducive to growth. Therefore, Donald Winnicott stated that for a baby to thrive into a healthy child, the caregiving just needs to be "good enough". In this way, the infant learns their caregiver is reliable and will provide for most of what they require in a satisfactory manner; not perfectly but satisfactorily.

If as an adult we have received this "good enough" parenting, we implicitly know we can depend upon another for our needs. We will have a balanced relationship to our needs and the needs of others. We are connected to our desires in an embodied way; identify them and ask for their fulfilment in a manner which is conducive to getting them met. If our needs are not met, we can self-regulate our emotions and communicate our disappointment, anger or distress in a way which maintains the connection in relationship.

Since our historical experience informs us that our needs are generally met, we implicitly know if at times we do not get what we want, we'll still be okay. Since we have this secure foundation, we are internally resourced and can maintain our emotional equilibrium when our needs are disappointed. Although we feel the disappointment of not getting what we want, we also understand this is not the *usual* and that next time we may get our need met. Or if it isn't exactly what we wanted, we can extract the good stuff and so experience it as good enough. We will also ask clearly for what we want, and if we need to be more specific or try a different approach, we will be flexible and do this. Furthermore, when our needs are not met straight away, we can delay gratification in a

healthy way. So rather than becoming overly demanding or dis-
missive of our needs, we can tolerate *waiting*, delay satisfaction
and know it may take time before our desires are fulfilled. These
internal resources are healthy and adaptive in adulthood, since not
all our requirements can be met all the time.

If however, at this second phase of development, we have not had
this "good enough" parenting, our experience with needs will be
very different. As an infant our needs feel *big* as we are completely
dependent upon someone else to meet them. We are not able to
regulate our emotional states or satisfy our physiological states by
our self at this stage. If then our need was not met, our emotional
arousal became greater as we protested the lack of response and
tried to communicate our requirement.[64] If our need continued to
be unmet, we became hyper-aroused. If still we were not responded
to, we eventually fell into a state of despair, finally giving up and
resorting to a more manageable state of arousal; hopeless detachment or hypo-arousal. We learnt therefore, that an unmet need results in extreme distress, disconnection and perhaps even feels life-
threatening.

As adults then, even though it is many years after, any inkling
of a need not being met (and re-experiencing of these feelings of
deprivation) may trigger our distress and feel very threatening to
us. This may occur even in very mild or seemingly innocuous situations. For example, we may become anxious when we are waiting for someone to arrive or to text us back on the phone. Such
situations often remind us of the time as an infant when we needed
something, but the person we depended upon did not respond in a
"good enough" way and so we felt increasing distress.

Thus, navigating the quagmire of needs can be a path fraught
with difficulty. We may become "unusually" upset and find it

difficult to regulate our emotions when our needs are not met. We could feel anxious, sad and angry, and perhaps even despair, hopelessness, deprivation and fear. Alternatively, we may criticise ourselves severely for becoming upset and think we shouldn't want anything.

~ ♥ ~

Survival Strategies to Avoid the Pain

Re-experiencing the feelings we had as an infant, when our caregiver repeatedly failed to attune and respond to our needs, is extremely painful. To avoid these painful feelings, we probably have a range of habitual and perhaps unconscious survival strategies.

These strategies are what our depleted/false self learnt to do to survive in an environment which failed us. As an infant, this protected our "natural being and aliveness" from annihilation. As an adult however, these strategies used by our depleted/false self can now thwart our growth towards wholeness and maturity. Our infantile pain longs to be understood, listened to and given the nourishment, care and support it needs. But if we continuously use our survival strategies to avoid it, it will remain unheard, deprived and depleted.

Let's now look more closely at these survival strategies, so we may gain some understanding about how we avoid this underlying pain. Broadly speaking and as alluded to previously, these strategies can be divided into three types; constantly seeking needs to be satisfied, cutting off from needs and focusing on another's needs.

One strategy we may engage in to avoid the pain of unmet needs is to be overly insistent; we may tend to engage in one-way relationships, expecting others to meet all our needs, but not truly seeing their needs in a reciprocal manner. This strategy can result in people eventually getting tired trying to meet all our requirements and so they eventually stop supporting us.

Whether conscious or unconscious, when we get an inkling this might occur, we start instigating a back-up plan. This is to avoid feeling the painful deprivation resulting from the lack of support.

For example, we may increase our demands and perhaps even use threats to get the other person to adhere. We might already have another relationship semi-lined up to fill the gap in support. Or we could check-out for awhile by numbing ourselves with alcohol, other drugs, prescription drugs, food, sex, work, entertainment or any other method we find useful to distract ourselves from our inner world.

A second strategy we may use to defend against painful feelings is rationalising we do not need much (or anything) from another person. Not relying on someone else to meet some of our desires means we can avoid the pain - rage, grief and deprivation - of unmet needs. We may become extremely self-sufficient or self-reliant, depending only on ourselves and non-human sources (e.g. books, food, work, alcohol, drugs) to satisfy us.

If this is our strategy, we may tend to react to our own needs and perhaps to the needs of others rather harshly. For example, we may turn away, ignore or become critical to any sign of our own or other's neediness. It is also possible we become anxious or angry with ourselves or others for desiring something. Basically, we devalue and disconnect from own needs and the needs of others. In this way, we stay clear of any possibility of our needs not being met, and thus avoid the pain associated with this.

Another strategy we might use, to avoid the pain of unmet needs, is to focus on meeting the needs of another. Our own needs here remain unconscious, but in a type of reversal, we consciously meet the needs of another, which (usually) mimic our unconscious desires. Our giving is not done freely. We give, but it's with unconscious strings attached. Although we would probably be appalled to admit, we care for other's needs to avoid our underlying pain and to get some of our own needs satisfied.

In infancy, we had no control when our parent did not respond to us. So now in reversing the situation and becoming the caretaker, rather than the one who needs to be taken care of, we establish full control. This allows us to keep the pain of the past out of awareness, as well as avoiding any present pain of our needs going unmet. Although we may get some second-hand satisfaction from meeting the other's desires, there is a cost to our caretaking, as again we do not get our true needs satisfied.

Perhaps we are hoping that if we fulfil the needs of the other enough, they will then care about us. Of course, whether this occurs is dependent on the person we choose to care for and their capacity to reciprocate. If we have never experienced a mutually caring relationship, it is quite likely we gravitate towards people unable to return our care, no matter how much we provide for them.

If this is one of the main strategies we use, we will eventually experience resentment at our own needs not being satisfied. The pain of unmet needs may then rise to the surface of our awareness. This may occur in two ways: We may literally feel aggrieved and angry at the other person for not reciprocating and/or not meeting our unconscious desires to be taken care of. Alternatively, since we give to get, our giving is usually loaded with our unconscious demands, which the other person will eventually feel (consciously or unconsciously). In this instance, rather than experiencing our own rage and resentment, we experience it via the other person, who eventually becomes enraged at our unspoken demands.

~ ♥ ~

Touching the Deprivation

If we want to work towards repair, we will need to touch the deprivation which occurred at such a young age. This includes the well of sadness and grief in our heart for what we missed, but so desperately needed. It also includes the deep-seated anger and rage stuck in our body. These are the intense feelings of the disappointed infant in us, who rightfully expected their basic needs of dependency (i.e. connection, care, support) to be met.

In touching these emotions as an adult, we may finally have compassion for the infant in us who needed someone to attune and respond to us. Like every infant, we needed someone to care for us; to provide us with what we needed, emotionally and physically, when we cried out or were frustrated.

We may begin to see more clearly the ways this occurred for us and the ways in which it didn't; allowing us to mourn what we missed. Here we eventually arrive at the realisation, it wasn't our fault. Just because the relational environment failed us in some way, it doesn't mean we (and our needs) were, or are, inherently wrong or bad.

Finally, in touching these feelings of deprivation, we will understand these emotions are not life-threatening anymore, compared to when we were so dependent. Accordingly, if some of our needs are not met now, we understand we will not (psychically or emotionally) die or collapse. We also understand we have some choice about how we go about getting what we need. We may then let go of the strategies our depleted/false self used to survive in our early life, and begin to take care of the real needs of the infant inside of us. In this way, these infantile parts of us have an opportunity to grow and become included in our wholeness.

In touching this deprivation, it is essential we do it in a way which is different from our early experience. We are gentle and kind. We allow it, rather than cutting off from it. We gradually step in and out of it, perhaps increasing the intensity over time, rather than allowing it to totally overwhelm us. Perhaps we practice delaying gratification of certain desires, so we can begin to tolerate the emotions that arise for us when we do not immediately get what we want. Here we learn to self-regulate our emotions when needs go unmet.

We also understand that distracting ourselves with other people's needs is not going to make our pain go away. Rather than engaging in indirect means to try and fill up our depletion and make ourselves feel better, we gain a healthy selfishness and become responsible for nourishing and caring for ourselves. In this way, we can then give to others from a sense of wholeness.

~ ♥ ~

Grieve the Loss

We must grieve the loss of missing out on someone being attuned and responding to us when we most needed them. It is important we allow someone in to see and hear this grief, rather than being alone with it. As an infant, we were alone in our grief and had to find a way to manage it on our own. So now we need a different experience. We need to grieve with another person who can sit and *be with* these feelings in us. Furthermore, grief requires a witness, just like when someone dies, they require others to acknowledge their passing, to feel the sadness of their departure and to say good-bye. We require a compassionate and attuned witness to acknowledge the loss of what we needed but did not get. We need assistance to recognise the ways we continue to adapt ourselves, while negating our real needs. Finally, we need this witness to validate and encourage our natural inclination to reach out for what we truly need.

Our tears bloom into compassion for our self and others. This is the beauty within grief.

Within this process of grieving, we need to understand it is too late to go back and get what we missed. We are no longer infants, entitled to be totally dependent upon someone who cares for all our needs. This realisation can be excruciatingly painful to grasp.

Right now in our life, although probably unconsciously, we may be trying to get back to that time, believing we would feel better if we just got what we missed. This may play out in various ways. Perhaps we continually search for someone who will take care of us, thinking we will feel better when we finally find the good attachment relationship we missed. Similarly, we may tend to avoid responsibility for our life, while wishing and hoping it will all just work out. In other instances, we might become dejected and believe we cannot do anything to change our situation, while hoping someone or something will come along and magically make us feel better.

Attempting to go back and get what we missed is not realistic, we are no longer infants and that developmental time has long past. We are now adults who are required to be responsible for our self. This insight can feel like a double punch in the guts. Not only did we miss out on what we needed to grow, now we need to grow up despite the fact we didn't get what we needed to do this. Therefore, it is important to get support in this process, for although we do need to grow up, we don't need to do it alone again. We can have nourishment, care and support through this.

Sometimes we will want this support person to save or rescue us from our pain. If we want to grow however, we need to take every step on our path. Our support person provides the "good enough" relationship, but they cannot take the steps for us or even carry us through it. Wanting to be saved will keep us stuck. We do require support, but feeling through the pain of our loss is our road to repair and our responsibility. Just like if we want to get fit, we are the ones who need to exercise. Indeed, no matter how much exercise our support person does, it will never make us fit. This is the same for the psychological process of growing-up we are doing here. We are the ones who need to engage in the process. Our support person provides the "good enough" relationship, walks by our side, encourages us and suggests what may be useful. But we need to take each step.

Embody the Rage

An infant requires their natural needs to be met. So if they are un-met, they feel anger and rage at the lack. As adults then, if our needs were not attuned to in a "good enough" way in this phase, we probably have unfinished business in regard to rage and our expression of healthy anger.

At this second phase in development the infant expresses rage in a very physical way, using their whole body. Hence, if we had to negate or restrict our expression of rage, we also probably re-stricted or froze our physical movements. Consequently, we may still have tightness in our shoulders, legs, back and joints. Body-work (e.g. massage, cranial sacral therapy, osteopathy), stretching, yoga, swimming and other relaxation techniques may therefore be important for us to soften, unwind and work through this tension.

We touch the rage to claim back the negated parts of our self.

Our feelings of anger and rage may be quite cut off and uncon-scious. Perhaps we think our anger is overly destructive and so we keep a tight lid on it, not wanting to express it as we believe it may destroy our self or the other person (when we are in relationship).

Eventually we will start to feel our anger and rage at the failures of our caregiver. We need to go through this process, not to blame someone else, but so that we can embody our natural enraged re-sponse to needs unmet and reclaim our right to need.[65] This is an essential factor in our repair.

Since rage is a very *energetic* feeling, we may need to embody it in a very physical way. If we think about this as integrating the warrior or warrioress inside of us, we may creatively come up with ways to express and allow this part of ourselves. For example, dancing wildly, practicing martial arts, boxing, weight training, beating our chest like a gorilla or roaring like a lion, are some ways we can playfully experiment with *touching* this feeling. A great example of a tribe of people who are practiced at integrating and expressing their warrior side are the New Zealand Maori. The Haka is an excellent physical example of a way to integrate the rage and fighting spirit of a warrior. Again, we can experiment here and have some fun in trying out different methods which may work for us. The essential point is that the emotion of rage is often expressed quite physically, so to *be with* and embody this big emotion, we'll probably need to include physical modalities in our integration.

Over time and with practice, safely stepping in and out of rage, we will gradually build up the strength of self to "be with" and embody the full expression of this emotion.

Through embodying our rage, we gain a healthy balance in our expression of anger. Most importantly though, we regain our natural right to need, understanding that just like everyone else in this world we can get our real needs satisfied.

Over time we begin to take a healthy responsibility for the fulfilment of our desires. We may begin by connecting to and knowing what our true needs are. Then asking directly and assertively for what we require.

If we do not get what we want the first time, we do not collapse into despair, self-hate, hopelessness or negate our need. We can *be with* the emotions which may arise, such as disappointment, sadness, anger or deprivation. Perhaps we alter the way we have tried to get what we want; implementing something else first or trying another strategy. Maybe we ask another person, do what we can ourselves or wait for the time to be more conducive. So rather than giving up and thinking it is hopeless, we have the strength and determination to persist.

~ ♥ ~

Taking in Nourishment

If the response to our needs, as an infant, was lacking, unpredictable or not conducive (i.e. toxic), then we may have difficulty *taking in* healthy nourishment and support now. Although we may feel the deep need for this nourishing support, particularly if we over-identify with this position, if we can't take it in, no matter how much we get, we won't be satisfied.

This might occur because we are more familiar with taking in inadequate nourishment. Perhaps we experienced such unpredictability in getting our needs met, that now it is difficult to trust that the nourishment will be enough and available again. Or maybe we are so familiar with taking in toxic nourishment that we keep gravitating towards this kind of support. This is a little like if we have only been exposed to junk food in our life. We do not understand this food is unsatisfying and not good for us. If we try some healthy food, it may at first appear bland or boring and so we go back to eating junk food, never quite understanding the difference between *good* and *bad* nourishment.

This same pattern will also occur in our relationships. Perhaps we don't trust someone will reliably support us. Maybe we engage in relationships which feel familiar, but do not emotionally nourish us. For example, we may be in relationships where the person provides for some of our practical needs (e.g. finances, housing, cooking meals, companionship etc), but emotionally is often distant, cold, controlling, dismissing, neglectful, manipulative, cruel or disrespectful. Since they are providing for our practical needs, we may "put up" with the neglectful or abusive emotional aspects of the relationship, not understanding the lack of emotional nourishment we are living in.

The issue of taking in nourishment is further complicated as we probably have a secret wish; to have the *perfect* type of nourishment. As a result, "good enough" nourishment doesn't always match up to our idealised expectations, thus it may seem not enough and unsatisfying. We might even think this "good enough" stuff is bad as it doesn't meet what we truly desire. So we continue to remain unsatisfied.

In reality there is no perfect source of nourishment. So if we want to feel satisfied, we will need to become familiar with taking in the "good enough" stuff. The infant inside of us will probably at times feel disappointed with what we get, as it doesn't match-up to our fantasy. However, if we can slowly let go of this fantasy of perfection and take in the *good* that is in the "good enough", we will experience some satisfaction. Although not perfect, it is okay.

If we are so familiar with no support, unpredictable support or toxic support, it may take us some time to distinguish between what is "good enough" for us, compared to what is familiar; seemingly normal, but NOT "good enough". Perhaps we start by becoming aware of what truly feels nourishing and what doesn't. We might then start to notice the differences between, something which feels good enough or supportive, something which feels toxic or unsupportive and something which feels lacking due to our fantasy of perfection.

We can be a little playful here, trying out different sources of nourishment and support while noticing how they affect us. For example, we might begin by comparing different ways we can spend our time. Does it feel nourishing to walk on the beach or in the forest, read a book, meditate, garden, cook, eat chocolate, swim in the ocean, watch a movie, do something creative, take a holiday on our own, have sex or make love, talk with a friend, spend time with family, spend time alone, sleep? Some of these ways to spend our time will feel deeply nourishing, while others will not.

In assessing what is truly nourishing for us, we may tune in and listen to ourselves, while we're engaged in these activities. Perhaps we notice what our body senses, how our heart feels, what our mind thinks and what our soul whispers to us. What we need, at any given time, does vary and change. So we need to tune into ourselves regularly; moment to moment and on a daily basis.

Sometimes our body needs to rest and relax. Sometimes it needs to move and stretch, dance, run, walk, ride or swim. Sometimes it needs to be touched, through massage, sex, hugging or holding hands. While at other times it needs hydration and certain foods. Our heart sometimes needs soothing, healing, love, kindness, protection and privacy, while at other times it feels nourished by fun, companionship, inspiration, openness and laughter. Our mind sometimes needs interest, stimulation, curiosity and variety, while at other times it requires quiet, calm, solitude and contemplation. Finally, the whispers of our soul are usually subtle, often not rational and do not abide by our earthly concepts. In heeding our dreams, longings and intuitions, we may begin to decipher the needs of our soul.

Our second step, once we have tuned in and listened to what we need, is to respond and act. We may begin in very small ways. For example, perhaps tonight we sense what would feel nourishing for our body to eat for dinner and so we cook it. We may then decide to carve out some time, during the week, to do something which feels nourishing for our heart and soul.

In this process of engaging in healthy ways to nourish and support ourselves, we will eventually need to move away from sources in our life which do not feel truly satisfying. This might include various habits we have (e.g. related to food, alcohol, drugs, etc), how we spend our time and certain relationships in our life.

Again, we will need to assess whether a particular source provides us with true nourishment, or whether we are making do and trying to get something good from something which is in fact not so good. The difference between eating fast food, compared to eating nutritious and healthy food, is again a good analogy for this. Although the fast food may taste good and initially fill our hunger, it does not do it in a complete and satisfying way, compared to healthy, nutritious food. This is the subtle difference we are required to discern. Fast food can be very tempting for its ease and instant gratification. We therefore need to slowly re-orientate ourselves, letting go of the fast food in our life and slowly integrate healthy and truly satisfying sources of goodness.

---

*Just like some foods feel nourishing to us
and others do not, some people feel nourishing
to us and others do not.*

Reciprocal Relationships

We will eventually move towards relationship with others in a mutually reciprocal way, where we are able to both give and receive equally. This is the final step in our repair.

To maintain reciprocal relationships, we need to balance the needs of our self with the needs of the other. How we get this balance, will vary amongst us, depending on the survival strategies we tend to utilise.

Some of us may be focused on trying to satisfy our needs and perhaps get anxious if our needs are not met all the time. We may benefit by realising we'll be okay if the other doesn't meet our needs every single time. We probably need to gradually tolerate our feelings of grasping, clinging, desire, wanting and hunger, without always trying to avoid or fill them straight away. In addition, if our needs are sometimes not met, it doesn't mean we are bad, unworthy or unlovable. If we have these reactions, perhaps we are required to develop some inner resourcefulness and confidence in our inherent goodness, worthiness and lovableness. We may also need to remind ourselves that since we are an adult now, we have many more options in how we satisfy our desires and can be more proactive in taking care of some of our own needs. Our journey requires us to gain a healthy balance between what others can provide us and what we need to provide for our self.

Some of us, on the other hand, are more self-reliant and have difficulty asking for and receiving support. We may benefit from understanding it is not a weakness to need nourishment, care and support from somebody else. This is a natural part of being human. It is healthy for us to reach out, be vulnerable and clearly ask for what we want. Since we probably don't ask others for much, we will need some practice in doing this. It will be important to ask people who will support us, rather than asking people who are familiar and show a history of being unreceptive and responding negatively. This is especially the case when we are first learning to reach out, as we need to experience what it is like when someone positively responds to us. And lastly, if we feel scared and that it is almost impossible to ask for our needs, we need to slowly build up the courage to risk reaching out to people we feel safe with. See box on the next page, titled, "I Feel Scared to Reach Out" for more detail about this.

Finally, some of us tend to provide for the needs of others, while sacrificing our own needs. We are required to become more healthily selfish and begin by giving to ourselves first. For us, this is how we get the balance of mutuality in our relationships. We will need to turn our focus inward, on what we need, rather than always outward and towards what others need. When we first start doing this, we may find it extremely difficult to know what we want, so we need to continuously practice tuning into our self. We may also feel selfish, guilty or that we are being overly indulgent by focusing on ourselves. We will need to tolerate some of these feelings, without going back to our usual ways of always focusing on others. Afterall, we can only truly give to others when we ourselves are nourished, supported and whole.

I Feel Scared to Reach Out!

Some of us may recognise our needs, but feel too afraid to reach out to satisfy them. We feel stuck between our longing and our inability to ask. This is a tricky position to be in. Here we are very close to our feelings of deprivation, longing and needing, but have no articulate strategy to get satisfaction.

Sometimes this is the case if we experienced our caregivers as frightening when we needed something. Our natural drive to reach out to be satisfied may have become fused with the more primitive drive to protect our self. These two drives are obviously quite different in expression. If we've had this type of attachment situation, we probably don't have a coherent strategy to get our needs met. In fact, we may blend a reaching out with a need to protect ourselves.

This need to protect may be exhibited by one or more of the general ways we react to fear. These include; fight (e.g. attacking the other and becoming angry), flight (i.e. avoiding and getting away from the other), freeze (e.g. becoming very still, dissociating, feeling blank or numb) and fawning (i.e. being overly solicitous or submitting to the other).

The drive to reach out and satisfy our need, and the drive to protect our self from danger (by fight, flight, freeze or fawn type methods), are incongruous. That is, when we need something (e.g. attachment, emotional support and safety) we naturally go towards people. However, this becomes complicated if when we go towards these people, our fear system is also activated.

What do we do, when we need something from a person, but also feel afraid and want to protect ourselves?

(1) Perhaps we approach the person with anger, in readiness to

fight and protect ourselves. That person may then feel like they need to defend themselves, rather than give us what we need.

(2) Maybe as we start asking for our need we are already fleeing away from the person. It is difficult then for that person to really hear what we need.

(3) Perhaps we become frozen, a bit like a deer in the headlights, so we are unable to speak coherently or in a dissociative way are extremely vague. This would make it difficult for the other person to clearly know what we want.

(4) Or maybe when we approach the person, we ask how they are and what they need, rather than say how we are and what we need. Obviously in this case, they will have no clue we actually need something.

In all these four scenarios, our reaching out to have our need satisfied has an approach-avoidance dynamic to it and is thus disorganised. Consequently, our reaching out is confusing. Furthermore, the other person may react to our fight, flight, freeze or fawn rather than our actual need. Then, not only does our need go unmet, but the other person's reaction to us may reinforce our fear of reaching out again.

If this resonates, it is essential for us to continue to take the risk to reach out. But, we need to do this with people we feel safe with and who are likely to listen and respond to us. We also need to understand that our reaching out, if paired with a fear response, is confusing. So we may need to prepare ourselves before we approach. For example, by calming ourselves, practicing how we might approach and what we might say. It may also be useful to explain to the other person our difficulty and fear of reaching out. When we repeat this experience with a person we feel safe with, over time, we re-learn that the drive to satisfy our needs doesn't need to be fused with the drive to protect ourselves.

Step-by-Step We Grow

If our relational environment was "not good enough", in this second phase of development, we missed some essential psychological steps. And so we are called to take them now.

Since the psychological work of repair can be difficult, we might believe we can skip some steps on this path. For example, we might think "I don't have to feel the deprivation or grieve the loss. It's in the past, so I am just going to change the way I do things from now on". We might believe looking back at our past is a waste of time as we cannot change it anyway. We might then decide to focus on the present, noticing and making changes from this vantage point.

This is a valid strategy; if we REALLY do this. When we REALLY focus on the present, the negated emotions from our past will come up in the present. So yes, we may connect and be with them, right here and now. If however, we say to ourselves, "This is from the past so I should just move on". And we don't take the time to be with the emotion. We are doing exactly to ourselves what was done to us as an infant. This type of strategy will not work, and simply reinforces the status quo.

Just like in building a house we need to lay the foundation before we can construct the walls; to grow into a secure and whole person we need to move through each stage, otherwise our inner (psychological) structure will be wobbly. This psychological process is a bit like when we learnt to walk and we progressed through a sequence of stages; sitting, crawling, standing, balancing, walking, then running, jumping and skipping with confidence. Each stage became integrated and acted as the foundation for the next. This is the same regarding our psychological/emotional growth.

On this path of psychological repair then, our first step is to understand the survival strategies we use to avoid our painful feelings. Then we can slowly connect to and be with the deprivation we avoid. In doing this we'll experience; not being destroyed, not being totally overwhelmed and not falling apart because of it. We may then truly grieve our loss and get in touch with our rage at needs unmet. In this way we reclaim our right to need, to take in nourishment and to be proactive in getting our true needs met. These are the steps we missed and are now required, one-by-one, to take.

If we are to become more whole, we need to take each step on this path. We cannot skip or gloss over certain stages.

Navigating this Path

On this journey of repair, it will be necessary for us to work through our deprivation, grief, rage and taking in of nourishment, with someone we feel is strong enough to support us and wise in their response to our needs. If we haven't had our needs met in a "good enough" way in the past, we may as adults gravitate towards relationships where again they are not met in a balanced and reciprocal way. Hence, for many of us with this legacy, it may be necessary to do some of this work within a therapeutic relationship.

In this therapeutic work, we may begin to integrate a healthier relational experience with ourselves and with others. In this process, which must be relational for true repair to take place, we come to know that our needs are normal and are a natural response to being human. We also understand, someone can be there for us when we need them, perhaps not every single time, but more than we have experienced in our life up to this point.

If our deprivation was severe, it may take time to become comfortable with someone responding to us when we ask for what we need. The fact that another is receptive, may be a truly foreign experience and one that we need to become more familiar with. If this is our first experience of receiving such responsiveness, it will probably also be coupled with large amounts of grief and anger, as we remember the contrast of our past when our needs were not met.

Along this journey we become connected to our real needs, gaining the strength to ask for their satisfaction in a clear way. Since we have learnt to self-regulate our feelings of deprivation, grief and rage, it is not catastrophic if our needs are not always met. Our strategies to get our needs satisfied become more flexible and conducive to getting the most beneficial outcome. Importantly, we can *take in* healthy nourishment and thus are satisfied.

This journey allows us to give and receive from a place of authentic vulnerability and authentic strength. In understanding and clearly asking for our needs, as well as being receptive to seeing and understanding the needs of another, we learn to sustain satisfying and mutually beneficial relationships. Indeed, there is the real potential here for shared give and take, rather than the one-sided dance we may have been living up to this point.

Growing up, just like giving birth, is a process of emergence where we struggle through a tunnel of unknown. In this tunnel we confront and connect to the lost parts of ourselves; all our pain and all our pleasure. This process of integration allows us to emerge into the light as the full human we were born to be.

My hope for all of us on this journey is that we have the courage to take each step through this tunnel. Including, touching the pain of deprivation, grief and rage we experienced at such a young age. This is where our growth lies and the path to our emergence.

Phase Three

A well-constructed house

(15 months to 3-4 years)

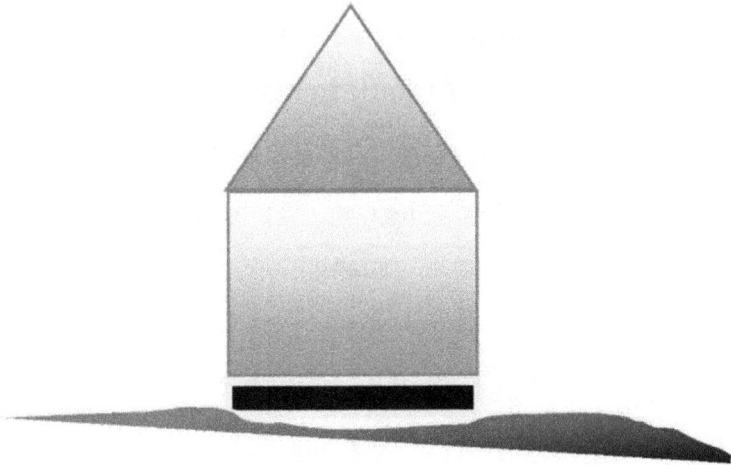

In our building metaphor, once we have secured the land and laid a sturdy foundation, we are now ready to build the house, brick by brick. This construction is analogous to the structure of our self. This is an important time in the psychological development of a child.

Development of a Separate Self in Relationship

It is okay to be me, with you

I am real | I am free to be me | I can be both vulnerable and

strong

In this third phase, other people apart from the primary caregiver become increasingly important to the developing child. In the first phase, the primary caregiver was the essential figure in the infant's world, with other caregivers acting in a support role. In the second phase, other people (e.g. father or other caregivers) start to become essential figures for the infant. Then in this third phase, as the toddler becomes increasingly separate from their primary caregiver, he or she looks to other regular figures in their life (e.g. the father, other caregivers, siblings, grandparents, aunties and uncles) to form attachments with. The community of people surrounding the child now take on a much more noteworthy role. This allows a smoother transition from the unity identity with the primary caregiver to a separate sense of self within various relationships.

This process of separation began in the second phase, for example via the slow weaning of the breast, and the infant being able to physically move away from their primary caregiver. However, the peak of this separation occurs in this third phase; the first major separation in psychological development.[q] Other major separation points occur in adolescence and then in early adulthood (in the early twenties). The issues surrounding each of these separations are slightly different, although the main theme revolves around identity formation as an individual in relationship with others.

This third phase heralds the *psychological birth* of the child; the formation and development of a separate self. It is commonly referred to as the "terrible twos", as parents remember the tantrums, the first words of "no" spoken and the insistence of their toddler

---

[q] I am not including the process of birth here, as although this is the most major physical separation from the mother, it should not be a major psychological separation. Psychological separation needs to occur slowly and over time, peaking towards the end of this third phase of development.

on doing things for themselves. It requires the parent and child dyad to negotiate much change, as well as conflicting desires and emotions. For example, on the one hand, the toddler wants to become more self-determining, but on the other, feels scared and overwhelmed by the demands of this and the increasing space of separateness. In a contradictory fashion, the child both wants something and doesn't want something. One moment they insist on doing everything for themselves. And then in the next moment seem almost infant-like in their frustration and distress, needing to be helped, soothed and held securely. It is these types of challenges which signal the significant developmental shift occurring for the toddler; the emergence of a separate sense of self.

In this phase, the toddler is visibly navigating their conflicting needs of dependence and independence, attempting to find a middle way in this dichotomy. If the child is assisted to navigate and find a balance between the two, they will grow to have a healthy sense of inter-dependence. They will understand it is okay to depend upon others and be vulnerable, as well as be self-determining and powerful. They will feel like they are free to be their real selves within relationship; spontaneous, creative and basically good.

At this time, the toddler needs to feel free to explore their world at their own pace. They also need to know they can go back to the safety and security of their caregivers at any time, to get the reassurance and re-fuelling they need, before they go off again. This requires a delicate balance, where the caregiver allows the child's growing autonomy, power and exploration, while also responding to their needs for security, connection, validation and reassurance.

Neuroscience informs us that between two and three years of age, a child's organic faculties (e.g. brain and nervous system) become more fully developed.[66] This is shown through increases in physical, motor, language and emotional-social development.

These increased abilities enable inner and outer conflict to be processed and resolved, allowing the identity of self to take greater form. For example, with increases in language the toddler begins to decipher "me and mine" from "you and yours", from "us and ours".[67] These developments also bring increasing complexity to relationships, with perhaps both understandings and misunderstandings increasing.[68]

The parent, in this third phase, is required to let go of the dream or idea they have of their child, and instead, allow for and nurture the *real* child within. In this way, the authentic and whole self of their child can emerge, just like a butterfly emerges from a cocoon.

For a butterfly to emerge, the caterpillar needs to go through a process of containment and struggle, to develop and emerge into its true nature. Without this containment (in the cocoon) and struggle (out of the cocoon), the caterpillar cannot become the butterfly it was born to be.

> *Both containment and struggle are necessary*
> *for the emerging separate self of the child.*

Containment in this sense means the caregiver can *be with* and *hold* both themselves and their toddler. This is specifically related to the full range of emotional states; from those which feel *good* to those which feel *bad*. Some of the emotions typical for toddlers, which require this presence and holding, include; grandiosity, entitlement, freedom, spontaneity, anger, frustration, disappointment, jealousy, helplessness and vulnerability.

Through the relational experience of the caregiver being with and holding such emotional states, in a balanced way, the toddler learns (through a process of identification) how to *be with* and hold their own emotional states.[69] Basically, the child learns the skill of regulating their emotions by; (1) seeing how their parent manages these emotions in themselves, and (2) how they experience their parent relating to the emotions in them.

When feelings are held and related to by the caregiver in a "good enough" way, the toddler learns how to hold, contain, understand and effectively express their emotions. If however, feelings are NOT held and related to by the caregiver in a "good enough" way, the toddler identifies with the "not good enough" way. For example, certain emotions are to be dismissed, controlled, criticised, judged, are overwhelming, need to be hidden, cannot be seen, are bad, etc. Basically, they learn some of their natural emotional states cannot be held, modulated or integrated into their whole self.

This is a dilemma for the developing toddler. On one side, the emotions they experience are simply part of their natural humaneness, or "being and aliveness". But on the other side, they are learning these natural expressions cannot be included in their whole *human* self. How does the toddler manage this discrepancy? As mentioned earlier in this book, a "false self" emerges to manage and adapt to this discrepancy. This false self complies with the external relational environment, while the natural expression of "being and aliveness" (in this case the expression of an emotion) is hidden and protected.

Within this overall sense of relational containment, the emerging self of the child also needs to push against, resist and struggle a little, to fully form itself and individuate. The toddler, at this stage, experiences this struggle at the interface of their internal world and the reality of the external world. This includes being frustrated by the discrepancy between their feeling of omnipotence and their testing of reality. That is, while feeling all powerful and in control, they begin to realise they cannot get everything they want from their caregiver and are not able to do everything they desire. This is further complicated by their growing awareness of separateness, and hence the realisation of their vulnerability and helplessness.

Consequently, a conflict for the toddler ensues. They want to regain the symbiotic intimacy with their primary caregiver, to feel secure. While fearing the loss of identity and independence such symbiosis entails.[70] This conflict is often outwardly displayed by a toddler in a "I need you" / "I don't need you" relational dynamic.

Although this can be challenging for the parent, the toddler is attempting to navigate an inner world filled with conflicting emotions. On the one hand, they feel frustration, anger, disappointment, confusion, angst, helplessness and vulnerability. While on the other, they are experiencing increasing competence, individuality, self-determination, realness, freedom, creativity and spontaneity.

This inner emotional turmoil, as already mentioned, needs to be met and held by a stronger and wiser attachment figure. The toddler requires their parent to "gently wrestle" with them in the external relational world, enabling them to successfully identify with the parental ego strength, emotional regulation, tolerance, patience and empathy. This allows the child to internalise and integrate these aspects of the "good enough" parent. It is in this way, they successfully wrestle with their own inner world.

This containment and struggle needs to be attuned and responsive to the child's emerging self; allowing for both self-determination and vulnerability and a balance between freedom and boundaries. It is through this "good enough" attachment relationship that the child is able to emerge into their whole individuated self.

Basically, relationship serves the same function for the toddler as the cocoon does for the caterpillar. The caterpillar uses the cocoon to emerge into the butterfly. In the same way, the parent must allow themselves to be used by their toddler, for containment and struggle, in service of the emerging self. It is only through a "good enough" relationship that the child is able to forge the ultimate balance of a separate self in relationship to others; enabling true psychological inter-dependence.[71]

Development can become stuck at this phase in two major ways: when the attachment figure, the child needs to be contained by and struggle with, is not enough (e.g. inadequate, weak, absent, fragile, permissive, neglectful), or alternatively when the attachment figure is too much (e.g. overpowering, tough, domineering, controlling, authoritarian, rigid, abusive). The difficulty for the child increases when their attachment figure displays these ways of relating, frequently and towards the extreme end. When both these relational dynamics are present, especially in the excessive amounts, say one parent is very permissive while the other is severely authoritarian, the difficulty for the child also increases. In the more severe cases, often both relational dynamics are present in the one attachment figure, where in some instances the parent is permissive or neglectful, while in others they are authoritarian or abusive. This type of attachment relationship is particularly confusing and disorganising for the child, as the parental response is unpredictable.

This phase requires the parent to engage in the ultimate balancing act, in service of the emerging self of their child. If the parent is absent, weak, fragile or permissive, the child does not have a strong enough attachment figure to feel contained by and gently wrestle with. The toddler then is unable to form or emerge fully from their infantile symbiosis, grandiosity and omnipotence. This is like a butterfly without the containment and resistance to be able to emerge successfully from its cocoon, and so it remains stuck; half in and half out. On the other hand, if the child is overpowered, domineered and controlled through this stage, the containment here may feel too restrictive and the struggle more like warfare than encouragement and support. This is like a butterfly who while in its cocoon has been prodded and poked; so it emerges either too early and hence not fully developed, or feeling like it has to protect and defend itself against attack. In both cases, the structure of the butterfly is compromised, impacting its ability to be true to its nature.

The Legacy

In "good enough" development we are generally loved and given attention for our whole self. We are cherished for who we are in all our glory; our grandiosity, ability to shine, to be self-determining and be the unique person we are, including our little quirks of being. And we are supported in our not-so glory; our frustrations, tantrums, infant-like ways, ambivalence, vulnerabilities and difficulties with big emotions. We are provided a balance of freedom/power and boundaries/limitations. And finally, our needs for both closeness and separateness are attuned to by our caregivers.

If this type of balanced and healthy recognition of our wholeness did not occur, in a "good enough" way, we were not able to emerge from our cocoon with a whole individuated self.

Consequently, parts of us remained stuck and unbalanced. We might now find it difficult to stand strong as an individual in relationship to others. Furthermore, our sense of self may swing from feeling too much (e.g. grandiose, strong, powerful, independent) to feeling too little (e.g. vulnerable, weak, powerless, dependent). It is also possible we express one side of this balance, while protecting the other. For example, we may exhibit our grandiosity and hide our vulnerability. Our legacy then, is an inner conflict between one or more of these opposites; grandiosity versus vulnerability, power versus powerlessness, dependence versus independence.

What this Means for Us...Now

If our whole self was unable to emerge in our early relational environment, we had to adapt and find a way around it, even if it meant our psychological growth was negatively affected. As adults, we may continue to disown aspects of our self we think are not okay; certain feelings, needs and desires. At the same time, we probably over emphasise aspects of our self we have learnt are acceptable. Generally, we continue to negate our wholeness and adapt to an idea of how we think we "should" be.

Our path here is one of authentic freedom. It involves discerning and embracing our *realness*, while letting go of the ways we adapt and betray our self. As we walk this path, we will be confronted with the task of individuation; standing as a separate person, while being in relationship with others. We will also be called to gain more balance in our sense of self; particularly in our grandiosity and vulnerability, power and powerlessness, independence and dependence. When we begin to integrate these opposing forces, we can then hold the inherent *ambivalence* in our self and in others.

In this section, I will begin by focusing on the false self. Even though this is relevant to all phases, I include it here as it is typically obvious in this phase.[r] I then discuss how we may balance the opposing forces specific to phase three: grandiosity/vulnerability, power/powerlessness and independence/dependence.

---

[r] See box on following page titled, "A Note on the Depleted/False Self".

A Note on the Depleted/False Self

The depleted/false self may begin in any phase of development. Basically, the earlier it occurs, the more hidden (and protected) the "natural being and aliveness" of the child (and thus adult) will be.

The *feel* of the depleted/false self for each person will vary. This variation depends upon the developmental phase it needed to come about, the specific failures in the relational environment it had to protect against and the survival strategies it had to use to adapt to these failures.

As a very general observation, the "depleted" aspect seems more recognisable when the relational environment in phase one and two hasn't been "good enough". While the "false" aspect seems more recognisable when the relational environment hasn't been "good enough" in phase three. This generalisation though is just a theoretical separation, as in reality it is a complex dynamic and thus cannot be spoken about in a definitive way. A more accurate statement would say that generally both depleted and false aspects are present when the relational environment hasn't been "good enough". And that the *feel* of the depletion and falseness, and the degree to which each are present, will differ depending on the relational experience of the individual in each of the phases.

Never-the-less, I feel the theoretical separation of the "depleted" and "false" aspect of the depleted/false self is important, mainly because the path of repair for each is slightly different. With the depleted aspect, we reconnect with our "natural being and aliveness" so our self arises from here; embracing our wholeness. Regarding the false aspect, we let go of this adaptation, understanding this is not our realness; there is more to us. Overall then, our repair includes a two-pronged approach; embracing our wholeness and letting go of the ways we have adapted ourselves.

The False Self

Although the path to becoming more whole requires much work, it is achievable. Perhaps the trickiest part of this process is that we'll need to understand and eventually let go of the false self.

Understanding the False Self

The formation of our false self was necessary for our survival. It allowed our "natural being and aliveness" to be protected, rather than destroyed or spoilt.[72] It also allowed us a way to function and cope in a world which couldn't adequately embrace our wholeness as a human being. However, rather than being who we were, we learnt what we should be; in order to survive and grow.

Our false self developed from the outside in. It looked to the external world to discern how it should be and adjusted itself accordingly. The image of a puppet is a good one, as the false self is similarly controlled by external strings, rather than an inner realness.

With this legacy, we will have parts of us which are not embodied in our real aliveness, feelings or needs. We will now generally fill this gap by trying to be a certain way; a bit like playacting. Consequently, we may struggle with knowing who we *really* are. And tend to present a certain image to the world, while negating our realness.

Like a puppet, the false self is limited in its ability to experience life, grow and flourish.

Since the false self doesn't arise from our "natural being and aliveness", it is secretly plagued by a lurking sense of emptiness or deadness. To fill up and hopefully feel better, it searches for external props and validation. This is essentially how the false self arose, so now it continues to need validation from the external environment to keep itself *alive* and know *how to be*. It also loves distraction; to avoid the emptiness and the painful truth of negating our realness as a human being.

With this legacy, we may find ourselves habitually searching or reaching for something, thinking, when I get there (or get it), I will feel fulfilled and everything will be better. What we imagine will make us feel better is individual and may include; having security, being cared about, meeting the right romantic partner, having a baby, being a good parent, having the ideal family, socialising with the right people, getting the right job or promotion at work, losing weight or having a more muscular body, becoming popular or liked, having a certain amount of wealth or power, being recognised for some achievement, going on exciting holidays, buying the latest tech device, meeting a certain spiritual teacher, becoming enlightened...and the list goes on. It is not necessarily the *thing* we are seeking which is problematic, but the place we are seeking it from. That is, when the desire to seek these things comes from our false self it will inevitably be a way to fill the void and thus be unhelpful in the long term. So the tragedy is, even when we do get to the place or thing, we imagined would make us feel better, it isn't long until we are searching again for something to fill the void and distract us from our real feelings and needs.

The false self is like a hungry ghost, never truly satisfied.

Our culture and world is complicit in this, so we think it is normal. For example, we are bombarded with the encouragement to consume; you need this to feel better is the implicit message in most advertising. So we think, for example, we need to keep up with the latest technology changes, to be well-read, cultured, intellectual, spiritual, to update our house for a better lifestyle, have the perfect body, get sexier clothes and have more radiant skin and hair; to feel okay about our self. This message to consume has become hypnotically embedded in our mind, diverting us from our real feelings and needs. Another way we fill up and ultimately distract ourselves, from our inner world, is through the constant stream of entertainment now available. Furthermore, being busy, juggling life, working and getting ahead in our careers to the point of being stressed and unable to relax, isn't considered problematic. On yet another front, social media has encouraged us to believe, being well-known, popular and liked, for our false self, is normal.

The point I am emphasising, is that we are surrounded by a social structure which makes it normal to continuously seek external validation. Furthermore, we are compliant with a social norm which encourages distraction from our real feelings and needs.

The problem with this, is external validation and distraction does nothing to solve the issue. We might feel better for awhile, when we get what our false self thinks it wants. But, it won't take long until we need to fill up again, because our false self is unable to give us what we are ultimately searching for; our realness and wholeness as a human being.

*We cannot distract ourselves from our lack
of wholeness, forever.*

Looking for an external fix, to resolve an internal problem, won't work. If we continue to seek outside of ourselves and avoid our real feelings and needs, we will keep on a constant merry-go-round; and get no-where. If we really want to feel better, we need to get off. That is, stop searching for external validation to feel okay, and begin connecting with our *real* being and aliveness. Put another way, separate from our false self's relentless standards and need for constant validation, and centre ourselves in our heart and soul.

But of course this is tricky. We have become so familiar with our false self that we might even think this is all we are. Consequently, we don't question this part of us, or fearfully think, "Who would I be without it?"

Becoming Curious about My False Self

In having the courage to question and become more aware of your false self, you may see how it is *useful* and how it *hinders* your wholeness. You may then understand this is just one aspect of yourself, not your total self; there is much more to you.

Here are a few questions to reflect on...

- When, how and with whom, do I adapt myself?

- What is this like for me?

- What am I afraid to show, feel and experience instead?

- What sort of external validation do I seek?

- How do I distract myself from my inner emotional world?

Separating from the False Self

Generally, we begin the process of separating from the false self when it isn't working for us anymore. Although we needed it to survive and cope, now as an adult it can be problematic and get in the way of living a fulfilling life. Our false self limits our experience of true connectedness to ourselves, others and the world around us. Consequently, we may experience dissatisfaction in our relationships, job, sense of meaning, enjoyment in life and being comfortable with who we are. We might also envy other people, who seem to have what we are missing.

These feelings of dissatisfaction and envy can alert us to how our false self has thwarted our true flourishing. For example: If we are dissatisfied in our relationships or envy people who seem to have close and fulfilling ones, perhaps our false self is sabotaging our ability to be intimate and connected. If we are dissatisfied in our job or envy people who find their work meaningful and satisfying, perhaps our false self is focused on striving to get somewhere, have more recognition, power or wealth, while ignoring the real desires of our heart and soul. If we envy people who get attention and recognition, perhaps our false self doesn't allow us to be attentive to our real needs. If we envy people who seem comfortable and contented in their own skin, perhaps the unrelenting standards and ideal image of our false self has approached its use by date, and it's time to become curious about who we really are.

Separating from our false self doesn't mean we need to get rid of it. It means we let go and stop clinging to the idea this is all we are. We stop allowing it to take over our entire being; choking our realness, aliveness and truth. We then employ the helpful elements of our false self, in service of our wholeness as human beings.

This is a bit like a gardener who differentiates the weeds from the flowers, manages the weeds and then provides nourishment for the flowers; allowing the garden to flourish. The false self is just one aspect of us; the part which has learnt, for better or worse, to function in the world we found ourselves in. If we want to flourish as human beings, like the gardener, we begin by discerning the difference between our false self and our *realness*. In other words, we notice the difference between disconnection and connection with our heart and soul. We then make room for our realness to grow, and provide the nourishment it needs to thrive. That is, we re-configure our life, so we live centred in our heart and soul.

Separating from our false self, connecting to our realness and thus becoming whole, will feel anxiety provoking and painful for us. This is due to two reasons.

Our false self developed to allow us to survive, as best we could, in the early environment we found ourselves in. We grew-up thinking parts of our "natural being and aliveness" were not okay, so to survive we negated these parts and adapted with a false self. Perhaps, as a child, there would have been serious consequences if we showed more of our realness. So our false self protected us from too much pain or humiliation, by hiding and negating it. Now as an adult we may fear giving our false self up, for we implicitly feel this part of us was essential for our psychological survival.

In addition, we may have been given special attention for our false self; being a certain way and playing a certain role for our caregivers. Basically, we got a payoff, in the form of attention, care and conditional love, for negating our wholeness and adapting our self. It is also possible we have been very successful in certain areas of our life, partly because of our false self. For example in our worldly achievements. To then give up this part of us, even if it doesn't feel authentic, will initially be coloured by uncertainty and feelings of fear. Since we have learnt the false self is who we are, to give it up raises a profound existential question: Who really am I?

This leads us to the second difficulty. When we start to see the false self for the adaption it is, we will touch the emptiness inherent in this disconnected part of us. It is possible we have been peripherally aware of this emptiness, but have steered clear of the uncomfortableness of experiencing it fully.

This however, is not the only difficulty. Underneath the emptiness of our false self, lies the pain of grief, anger, loss and fear.[73] This pain relates to the initial reasons we adopted this self. It is the pain of not getting what we needed in a "good enough" way. It is also the pain of having to negate our wholeness; early in our life and then throughout our life.

This is the double whammy we are afraid to face. Firstly, separating from the part of us which helped us survive and get to where we are. Secondly, touching the inherent emptiness of our false self and experiencing the underlying painful feelings.

~ ♥ ~

Entering Emptiness:
Embracing Pain (and Joy)

To walk this path of repair, we need to look our false self squarely in the face, and recognise its inherent emptiness and disconnection from who we really are. At the same time, we need to gently embrace the underlying pain (and joy). This is the way through to the discovery of our wholeness.

Contacting the emptiness is initially frightening. Since the false self is disconnected from our "being and aliveness", without it we could feel like we are nobody. To avoid this fear, we continue with our familiar false ways. We figure it's better to be somebody, even if it doesn't feel fulfilling, than nobody. We do not understand that through this emptiness, if we just sat with it for awhile and within the darkness allowed it to be, we would touch our "being and aliveness".

This however can be tricky. As underlying this emptiness, is the pain (and joy) negated and inherent in being a whole human being. Whether we like it or not, we cannot have joy without pain; since they arise from the same source. If we negate, numb or avoid our pain, we also negate, numb and avoid our joy. Our wholeness includes the embodiment of both pain and joy. If we want to be whole, this cannot be avoided.

Navigating the emptiness and embodying the underlying emotional pain and joy, is the way through to our realness.

Separating from our false self, entering the emptiness and embracing the pain and joy of our wholeness, needs to be done slowly, gently and with nourishing relational support. We do it, bit by bit, over time. The timeframe I am alluding to, generally, is over many years. There is no rush and no hurry. In fact, rushing this process is counterproductive, and probably based on the impatience of our false self wanting to get somewhere or be someone. This journey towards becoming fully human has no such time frames. Within nourishing relational environments, our wholeness can be discovered, grow and mature over our entire lifetime.

This work also needs to be done in tandem. That is, we work on separating from our false self and at the same time begin to connect with the pain and joy of our wholeness (i.e. our "natural being and aliveness"). This includes separating from relationships, activities, beliefs and goals which serve our false self. At the same time, we identify and begin engaging in relationships, activities and goals which nourish our heart and soul.

Giving up the false self too quickly, without some basis in our "natural being and aliveness", will leave us without a place to land. This is when we become terrified and possibly even experience suicidal thoughts. The loss of our false self here has been too sudden and abrupt. If this occurs, we probably need to seek assistance to find our feet again. It is also essential to remind ourselves, this path is a gradual one, taken step by step. There are no sudden breakthroughs, shortcuts or quick fixes.

Symbolically, letting go of the false self can feel like a death of sorts. While re-connecting to our "natural being and aliveness" is like a process of resurrection. In essence, one part of us goes through a death process, while another part goes through a growth process. Consequently, the archetypal themes of death and re-birth (or resurrection) may be felt at various points on this journey.

Stepping into the emptiness and pain is the way through to becoming whole. We allow all parts of our self to be included; with kindness.

This is not easy. Our false self generally doesn't want to acknowledge the parts it thinks are ugly, disgusting, childish, immature, unpleasant, bad and negative. These are the labels we learnt to give the aspects of ourselves we hide and negate. However, if we take a wider perspective and stop maintaining the image our false self seeks, we begin to understand these parts are simply *human*.

Rather than rationalise, ignore, reject or attack these negated parts of our wholeness, we acknowledge they exist and are parts of us (and a part of all humans). Like everyone else and everything else on this earth, our wholeness encompasses good and bad, positive and negative, dark and light aspects. It does not make more of one side and less of the other, criticise one side and perfect the other, or idealise one side and devalue the other.

The challenge we face on this path is to embrace the opposites we find within ourselves (and others), with kindness and equanimity. This sounds simple, in theory. In reality, it is the work of the warrior and warrioress.

Wholeness includes every-thing and
no-thing.

Becoming Whole

Our whole self develops within relationship; arising from our "natural being and aliveness". This is akin to an organic process which cycles through times of growth, death and maturity. And which can only be achieved within a nourishing relational environment.

Our "natural being and aliveness", is the essence of who we are. It has always been. So on this path of wholeness, rather than construct something else or try to change something about ourselves, we go through a process of re-emergence. Basically, we go back to the place we got stuck in our development, and from that point begin the process of growing up again. But this time we do it in a relational environment which facilitates the emergence of our whole self. As mentioned previously, this process has two intertwined elements: (1) We re-discover and re-connect to our "natural being and aliveness", so our self may arise from here. When this occurs, our self is not depleted. (2) We let go of our false self.

This path includes stepping into the unknown territory, often referred to as the hero's journey,[s] to realise who we really are. It is like wading through mud on a dark night, to find the gold; our innate "being and aliveness", which we emerge from and then bring into the world. This requires skilful effort, a guide to show us the way and trust in the process. Like all the mythological legends warn us, it can be a difficult journey, but certainly possible.

My sense is that every single person needs to go through this process, to a greater or lesser degree. This may be a fairly simple

---

[s] Term coined by Joseph Cambell in Campbell, J. (1949). *The Hero with a Thousand Faces.* United States: Pantheon Books.

process for some. For others it will be more arduous, difficult and painful. And for a few of us, the prospect of moving through the pain inherent in this journey will be initially unthinkable.

If however, we don't eventually build the courage to attempt this hero's journey, we will continuously need to find ways to avoid the emptiness and pain. This is a desperately sad scenario as it is impossible to do this successfully or completely. With no basis in our "natural being and aliveness", our false self will always have a sense of emptiness. So if we carry on living from this part of ourselves, we will continue to be plagued by meaninglessness and dissatisfaction. Even if our false self seems to be "having a whale of a time", its inherent emptiness and disconnection from our heart and soul, will always whisper to us. It can be no other way.

If we continue to avoid or fight against the emptiness and hidden pain, we will forever be stuck in a never-ending cycle. This is like putting a band-aid on a crack in our ceiling to stop the water leaking through. The water will eventually seep through. Perhaps not in the place the crack was, but it will find a way, and in the process cause a lot more damage than was ever foreseen.

When we live from our "natural being and aliveness", our experience of self, others and the world is different, compared to living from a false self. Perhaps a good analogy is like when a person addicted to cocaine comes off it and begins to live an ordinary life. Life can initially feel boring and mundane, compared to the ups and downs of the drug or false lifestyle. Like a drug, the false self can be seductive in its promises. And like an addiction, it thrives on a roller-coaster of highs and lows.

In connecting to our "being and aliveness" and becoming whole, life does feel more ordinary. But it has depth, stability and most of all it is real. The joy is real, the pain is real. It is felt, it is experienced. We now have two feet firmly planted on the earth. Clinging to the ideal standard of our false self reduces. We stop avoiding our pain and hoping for something to make us feel better. Over time, we feel more relaxed, calm and contented. Life begins to take on more hue and colour. We begin to enjoy the extraordinary found in the ordinary moments of every day.

~ ♥ ~

Balancing Opposites

On this path towards wholeness we begin to integrate opposites; acknowledging the good and the bad simultaneously. This includes, grandiosity and vulnerability, power and powerlessness, independence and dependence. Over time, rather than idealising one and devaluing the other, we realise wholeness embraces both sides; allowing room for ambivalence in our sense of self and experience of the other.

Balancing Grandiosity and Vulnerability

In the developmental process of forming a self, we experience our uniqueness and grandness, a little like being the king or queen of our world. In juxtaposition, we are also in touch with our intense vulnerability as a human being.

In this third stage of growing up, we required a balance of admiration for our magnificence and validation of our human vulnerabilities. If our caregivers were able to hold and balance both these sides, we grew to include both aspects into our self. This allows us, as adults, to experience both our glory and vulnerability. We can acknowledge our uniqueness and worth, as well as our ordinary humanness.

It is of course impossible, for a caregiver to get the exact balance of this holding right all the time. Consequently, as adults, we all probably have some unfinished psychological business here. Again, if our caregivers were generally "good enough" with this balance, then we will have greater security and wholeness in our sense of self, (including a balance in our gloriousness and vulnerability). If however, our caregivers had more trouble holding and negotiating this balance, we probably acknowledge one side, while negating the other. We might even swing, like a pendulum, from one side to the other. So rather than feeling balanced and secure, we feel somewhat fragile and insecure in our self.

This balance, in our grandiosity and vulnerability, generally goes awry in three possible ways. We may have been provided with (a) too much for healthy development, (b) not enough, or (c) given the opposite or wrong kind (e.g. humiliated/shamed, rather than recognised for our magnificence and validated for our vulnerability).

In the first instance, we may have been provided with too much recognition for our strengths, magnificence, entitlement and specialness, without any reality checks about our limitations and ordinariness. If this was the case, we probably acknowledge our importance and worth, but are unaware of our weaknesses and the fact we are subject to the limitations of being human. Perhaps the satisfaction of living an ordinary life is not enough for us. Furthermore, we might feel entitled to and thus expect constant admiration, special treatment and external validation for our "greatness".

On the other hand, perhaps it was our vulnerability and weakness which was overly validated, without a corresponding recognition of our strengths. This sometimes occurs if we were often sick, had special needs or if one of our caregivers needed us to be dependent. In this case, we may over-identify with our human fallibility. Perhaps we form an entitled self-image concentrated on our weaknesses and limitations, while disavowing our strengths and capabilities. Thus, we might expect special treatment for our fallibility and become enraged when others don't continually make concession for us.

Something slightly different occurs, in the second and third instances, if we were ignored or shamed. So on the grandiose side of the balance, perhaps our need for admiration was ignored or shamed. For example, we may have grown up in a family where a healthy sense of entitlement was equated to being "big headed". Perhaps we were teased about our natural grandiosity and need for admiration. Or there was no-one who recognised and delighted in our uniqueness. Consequently, we may negate the entitlement of the king or queen inside us. We may however, make up for this apparent lack by working hard to prove our worth and value. For example, we might strive for excellence in a certain field or want to be recognised in a particular manner. The ways we do this are many and varied. Some examples include; being extra helpful, charitable, responsible, giving, funny, pleasant, adaptable, smart, wealthy, powerful, famous, studious, competitive, shrewd, talented, creative or social. It is the sense of striving to prove and get recognition for our self-worth which underlies this position, rather than the specifics of what we do.

On the other side of the balance, perhaps it was our vulnerability which was ignored or shamed. If so, we may have a difficult internal relationship to this part of ourselves, or possibly not in touch with it at all. Perhaps some of our feelings were ignored, mocked, received with disgust and anger, or turned away from. Maybe our caregivers expected more of us than we were capable of, so we tried our best to fake it, so we wouldn't upset or disappoint them. Consequently, we might have a kind of toughness about us, hiding certain aspects of our vulnerability, while outwardly disavowing our sensitivities, weaknesses or limitations. Unlike the person who was given too much admiration without any reality checks and believes they are unlimited, we think if we show our vulnerability we will be attacked in some way (e.g. humiliated or criticised). So by hiding, camouflaging or disavowing this part of ourselves, we protect our vulnerable self from exploitation, manipulation or shame.

In reality, we might have a mixture of all these possible imbalances. This mixture can vary depending on the situations we are in and the people we are with. Our individual matrix therefore can be multifaceted and changeable. Given this however, we probably have certain leanings towards some more than others. It may be useful for us then, to take some time to reflect on the leanings we specifically have.

When we include both grandiosity and vulnerability, in a balanced way, our self becomes more whole and secure. If we think of a traditional weighing scale, the two sides need to be equal for it to be stable. If the sides are not equally balanced, it will be weighed down by one side, or sway from one extreme to the other. This is the same with our self, when the two sides of these opposites are unbalanced.

Rather than doing the work of integrating these two sides of us, the false self tries to gain stability by living up to an ideal image (e.g. of perfection, power, likability and invulnerability). Since we encompass both strengths and weaknesses however, we inevitably fall short of this image. Indeed, the inherent nature of all form, including our human form, is the play of opposites (e.g. dark and light, good and bad, yin and yang). Essentially, if there is no opposite, there is no form and thus no human being. So like every other formation on this earth, we human beings consist of opposing forces. However, since the false self is disconnected from our essential humanness (i.e. "natural being and aliveness") and lives from an ideal image, it struggles against this play of opposites by over-valuing one side and devaluing the other.

When our false self is confronted with the side of our wholeness it has devalued, it will experience shame, anger, disgust or despair. This may occur within us or in relation to another. It may then criticise this aspect and think I am (or you are) less than and perhaps even worthless. The false self thinks the reason it feels "bad" is because it (or the other) has fallen short of its ideal image. To feel better, it then tries to re-instate this ideal image.[74]

The same process occurs when the false self is confronted by an aspect of wholeness it has over-valued. In this case it may feel pride, self-righteousness, superiority or euphoria. Again, this may occur within us or in relation to another. The false self believes the reason it feels "good" is because it (or the other) has lived up to its ideal image. Thus, it will work hard to maintain this image.[75]

So the roller-coaster continues, of trying to maintain and live up to an image which is disconnected from the reality of our actual *felt* experience. To step off this roller-coaster, we need to separate from this false way and balance all aspects of our wholeness. For a step-by-step guide on how we may start this, see box titled "Becoming Balanced".

In summary, our path here includes the integration of opposites. That is, we begin to recognise and hold opposing forces. For example, good and bad, love and hate, strong and weak, unique and ordinary. Rather than inflate one side and reject the other, we recognise and embrace the two sides of our "being and aliveness". This allows us to become whole and human. Then when we acknowledge that every person contains these opposites, we allow those around us to be whole and human too.

Becoming Balanced

Step 1: Start noticing when you devalue or over-value

(a) Perhaps you become aware of when you *devalue* or *under-emphasise* aspects of yourself or another. You are alerted to this when you feel a strong negative reaction, (e.g. shame, embarrassment, anger, irritation, disgust) and tend to repress or disconnect from this part of yourself (or the other). If someone so happened to question your "negative" perception, you may feel resistant, not want to take in what they are saying or think they don't understand. Generally, you want to maintain your one-sided perception, so it'll take courage to acknowledge your devaluation.

(b) You may also start to become more mindful of when you *idealise* or *over-emphasise* an aspect of yourself or another. The idealisation will have a strong positive reaction attached to it (e.g.

---

pride, self-righteousness, superiority or euphoria). You may feel a magical sense of connection, a heightened sense of power and in- vulnerability, a sense that this is perfect or a rapid rise in your self- esteem. In addition, if someone so happened to question you about the validity of your "positive" perception, you would probably have a strong negative reaction to them or perhaps think they "just don't get it". Again, you are invested in maintaining your idealised position, so it'll take a dose of reality to acknowledge that maybe you are seeing things in an overly positive way.

Step 2: Acknowledge you are only seeing one side of the coin
When you have tipped the balance of opposites to an overly nega- tive or positive position, you are seeing and experiencing one side, without a balance of the other side.

Step 3: Take some time to sit and contemplate
Here you may, (a) connect with the part of yourself that you have under-valued or over-valued. That is, really touch the physicality and emotional aspect of it. Be with it and embrace it fully. Then notice what occurs. A more detailed explanation of this process can be found in PART III, under the heading *"Being With" Emotion.*

Alternatively, you may, (b) contemplate the opposite. For ex- ample, if you idealise your (or someone else's) strength, you may then contemplate the weaknesses or limitations you (or they) may also have. If it is your limitations you are more in touch with, you may then contemplate the strengths. It will then be useful to reflect on both aspects (e.g. the strength and the limitation) and begin to acknowledge, connect with and embrace both sides. Over time you understand that both sides are necessary for wholeness.

Step 4: Embrace your experience

You work to embrace your (and the other's) wholeness. This includes the parts you feel embarrassed, irritated, appalled or disappointed by, as well as the parts you feel proud of, entitled to, and take pleasure and joy in. Your embrace occurs physically and emotionally, so this aspect of you can become embodied and thus integrated into your sense of self (or your experience of the other).

It is important to note that the actual part you embrace (i.e. whether it is the under-valued or over-valued aspect) is not of the greatest importance. The most essential thing to remember is the actual process of embracing. When you truly embrace (both physically and emotionally) an aspect of yourself, you will naturally begin to contact your "being and aliveness". Since your "being and aliveness" encompasses both sides and is underscored by a sense of equilibrium, you will feel more balanced, stable and whole. This process of embracing (physically and emotionally) whatever you are experiencing, is not necessarily easy, but it is the path to wholeness.

Step 5: Talk to someone you trust

It may be beneficial to speak with someone about this process you've just been through.

Power, Control and Will

During this third phase of development, we gradually recognise that we are separate from our caregiver. We begin to understand we do not control or have power over another person. Consequently, the illusion the other knows exactly what we want, and can give it to us, exactly when we want it, becomes disillusioned. This adjustment to reality is often accompanied by disappointment, frustration and anger. Simultaneously, we are also recognising we have our own mind and will, separate from our caregiver. Our experience of this is felt as powerful, exhilarating and a little frightening.

To successfully navigate this stage, as a child, we needed our caregivers to optimally indulge and frustrate our feelings of power, control and need for self-determination. Too much indulgence, where we were the most powerful one in the relationship, (e.g. getting what we want whenever we wanted it), meant our power, control, will and anger were not balanced nor modulated. We may have felt too powerful and able to control the will of our caregiver. This amount of power would've felt somewhat frightening as a child, as we were not held in our strength. Likewise, excessive frustration or subjugation of our power and will, by our caregivers (e.g. rigid rules, harsh discipline, not being allowed to make some of our own choices), meant we were denied our own freedom and self-determination. In this case, as a child, we probably felt powerless, trapped and controlled by the will of our caregiver.

When this phase is transgressed successfully, we understand the balance of our power and will. We know we are not all-powerful and control the world around us, neither do we experience ourselves as powerless, with no rights or sense of agency in the world.

We feel free to make our own choices and allow others to make theirs. We understand that compromise doesn't mean one person has to give-up who they are, but is a way to allow disparate needs to be included and met where possible. We also understand other people have an inner world of their own, separate from us. Therefore, we engage in relationships with reciprocity of give and take, neither the giver all the time or the taker all the time. We also feel free to be authentic in relationship and allow others the freedom to be authentic too.

Many of us have unfinished business related to this theme of power, control, will and freedom. Like a coin has two sides, there are two ways we may display these; overtly and covertly. Often we are more familiar with one side. Although the other will also be present, but perhaps in a more subdued fashion. Let us explore these two sides in a little more detail.

Firstly, we may overtly or openly be in touch with our power and will. Perhaps we experience ourselves as the most powerful one in comparison to others. This may occur in our workplace and/or personal relationships. It is possible we like being in control, to be all knowing, to be the boss, to feel superior, or to be unquestionable. Perhaps we expect others to adhere to our expectations and do as we say. In addition, we might secretly think we are limitless and not subject to the normal laws of reality. In fact, we could get quite a shock when confronted with certain givens of life, such as sickness, aging, loss and death. Finally, it may be easy for us to harness our will, and drive ourselves (and others) to get what we want. We are also probably closely in touch with our feelings of anger, which can act as a motivating force for us. Finally, we may at times be a bit of a bully, using our anger to control others and get what we want; like a bull pawing the ground with its hoof.

The second way this theme may present in our lives is in a more covert or hidden manner. Here we may feel powerless and a lack of freedom to be who we are. We may consistently experience ourselves at the hands of more powerful others, perhaps even feeling we have no choice but to submit to their control and will. Maybe we think there is no point in trying, exerting our will or that there is little hope of change, since the other's rights, needs and desires are so much bigger, tougher and more important than our own. Consequently, we may suppress or disconnect from our will, desires and drive. Our anger may smoulder in the background, showing up as depression, passive-aggressiveness or resentment, rather than outward aggression. These feelings may also be used to control others, but this time we do it by withholding; like a donkey determined not to move.

With unfinished business here, we are firstly required to understand the limits of our power, control and will. For example, we cannot control other people; their nature, decisions or reactions. We do not have power and control over some events which occur in our life, including the fact that one day we will die. Like death, there are many unknowns in life, which we cannot control. As we age, our skin will become wrinkled, we will feel less able physically, our hearing and eyesight may reduce and we'll have less potent energy. These are the limitations of our human body, eventually leading to death. Furthermore, throughout our life, we will be subject to many other events which are out of our control. For example, we will become sick and then well again, we will have many joys and disappointments in our relationships, and we will experience numerous beginnings and endings in different spheres of our life. These aspects of life will occur; they are part of living and being human, and we cannot escape them.

The second aspect we are required to understand about our power and will, is that we do have agency and some choice in our life. Although we cannot control our nature, the nature of other people and the nature of life, we have many choices regarding how we navigate this terrain.

If for a moment, we think about ourselves and our life like the ocean. We cannot control how the ocean is from one day to the next; sometimes it is wild with large waves, while at other times serenely calm. Since this is the nature of the ocean, of us and of life, although we cannot control it, we can learn to navigate it. For example, we may spend effort in learning to swim in different waters, rather than in wishing the ocean was a certain way. We may also make choices about when and where we will go into the water, and whether we sometimes remain dry and watch from the shore.

In practical terms, in our life, we may exercise some choice in the following areas; the values which are important to us, how we live our life, the way we earn money, the way we spend our leisure time, the people we choose to have relationships with, how we manage our finances, health and psychological wellbeing, our interests, the food we eat, the music we listen to, and the list goes on. Within all these categories there is not necessarily unlimited power and choice, but within each, there is a *degree* of power and choice we can determine for ourselves.

Overall, we usually run into trouble when we try and exert our power and will in areas we don't have control. If we do this, we will probably feel angry, frustrated, wound-up and enraged. And have a sense of spinning our wheels and getting no-where. We will also get stuck and run into trouble when we don't exert our power and will in situations where we can have some influence. If we reject our ability to be self-determining, we will become despondent, depressed, despairing and hopeless.

Our power, control and will are not always easy to navigate. It can be tricky, as what we want may conflict with the limits of existence, our human limits or the desires of other people. Consequently, it is likely we'll be confronted with these themes throughout our lives, particularly within our varied relationships.

The complexity of these themes increases when we consider the paradox of our human journey. This includes the paradox of living within the limits of reality as a human being, while knowing our heart and soul is less defined by these limits. It also means understanding that since we have our own body and mind, we are separate from others, while at the same time and in the deepest sense we are inter-connected. Consequently, we are learning to balance our power and will, with the power and will of others, while deeply understanding our inter-dependence.

As a human being living on this earth, we are inter-dependent - with other humans, all other species and the natural environment.

Inter-dependence

Within this third stage of growth, we begin to balance our dependency on others with our need for self-determination and independence. This equilibrium however, can be tricky to attain. Often we struggle throughout our lives, with one side of the balance showing up as more prominent than the other. This struggle is most easily seen in our relationships, especially when we interact with someone who has a different balance to us. For example, many classic conflicts in intimate relationships arise because of one person trying to get their needs of dependency met (e.g. wanting more intimacy and support), while the other person struggles to get their needs of independence met (e.g. pursuing their own interests and time alone).

Competing needs, just referred to, also occur in the child and caregiver dyad. However, since children literally require their caregiver to survive and grow, as a child, we would've adopted the degree of balance which was most comfortable for our caregiver. If we were lucky enough to have caregivers who embodied a balance of both dependence and independence, then we probably have a greater ease balancing these two sides. If however, their balance was more towards dependency, we may have felt nurtured by the relationship, but also a little stifled by it. If our need for self-determination wasn't as encouraged, although we may now feel supported in relationship, we might be unconfident when wanting to do something (or be) on our own. On the other hand, if our caregiver's balance was more towards independence, we probably now feel quite confident in our sense of self-determination and agency. However, we might not value our dependent needs, particularly the nourishment relationships afford.

Some of us may have grown up with a parent who needed us to be what they wanted for their own dependent needs, rather than allowing us to be true to our self, including our independence. Perhaps they wanted us to be close to them and felt better when we did not explore too much, just in case we got hurt. Maybe our differing opinions, ideas or thoughts, threatened them, and so we stifled our individuality. Maybe they wanted us to care for some need in them, and so we remained close to quell their fears; for example, of aloneness or emptiness. Perhaps we felt caught in the middle of our parents, acting as the decoy for their conflict or lack of relationship. If any of these scenarios were the general theme in our childhood, we may have had difficulty exploring the world on our own and separating from our caregivers.

As adults we may be sensitive to the relational needs of others. We might even shape ourselves according to the desires of the other and be particularly flexible, adaptive and charming. It is also probably important for our self-esteem that other people like us. Consequently, if a person we have been trying to "win over" doesn't succumb to our charms in the way we would like, we could feel wounded, abandoned or even worthless.

Our familiarity with dependence however, could be stifling to the part of us which wants to be an individual. We may struggle with independent action, not feeling free to explore and be ourselves. Generally, we probably rely heavily on another for our sense of feeling okay and perhaps think without them we wouldn't amount to much. This may mean we have difficulty making decisions and look to others for advice, opinions and to solve problems. We probably also are not confident to explore the world on our own. Perhaps we then stifle our curiosity and excitement about what we want to do, or alternatively persuade the other to go along with us.

The thought of being alone might terrify us, so we make sure we stay close to people. This could mean we quell our inner voice when we want to try something apart from others. We might even become anxious or scared about pursuing things on our own or doing something that feels true to us. This will especially be the case if we think it might upset or disappoint the other. Perhaps we are sensitive to and fear any separation in a relationship, so we make sure the connection stays on an even keel, without conflict, even if it means not being who we really are.

Breaking down the illusion of non-separateness probably feels anxiety provoking to us. So to reduce our separation-anxiety, we focus on the other at the expense of our own self-determination and true needs. We may however, feel an underlying anger about giving up our independence. This probably mostly simmers under the surface, perhaps expressing itself in depression, resentment, passive-aggressiveness or subtle control of the other.

Conversely, it may have been the other way for us. Maybe our caregivers required us to be prematurely independent. Perhaps they were busy, stressed, pre-occupied or felt uncomfortable with our dependency needs. Thus, it served their purposes for us to be more quickly self-sufficient and not rely on them. If this was the case, we were probably encouraged to grow in our independence, while learning to quell our needs of dependence. Consequently, we may have missed a person being there for us when we needed to emotionally re-fuel.

It is likely we appeared to be exploring our world, in much the same way as a child who is provided a "good enough" balance of independence and dependence. However, we probably found ways to manage our own distress, without seeking the reassurance or emotional soothing found in relationship. If there wasn't someone there for us when we needed them, we learnt to push our natural feelings aside and depend on non-relational sources to soothe us. We probably put energy into negating our dependency needs, knowing we couldn't get them met by our caregivers.

As adults, we may be very capable and accomplished at what we do. We may focus on achievement, work, pursuit of leisure, material acquisition, prestige or power, as the most important aspects of our life. We are most likely quite successful in our work, our accomplishments and the life we appear to live.

In this position we have negated our need for others. Consequently, we probably have some difficulty with closeness, intimacy and relationship. We may not allow ourselves to be vulnerable, ask for help or be comforted by others. And probably, we find ways to self-soothe rather than go to another person when we need support. Without the balance of being able to rely on our relationships, particularly in an emotional way to feel secure and soothed, we can also become a little hard-hearted towards ourselves and others.

We may seem tough and appear quite strong to an outside observer. It is quite likely we also highly value independence and want to remain strong. We might even think we are weak if we need relational and emotional support.

If someone gets too close to our emotional vulnerability, we could react with outward anger, aggression, blame or dismissal. In this way we keep ourselves and others away from the pain of our unmet dependency needs, and thus allow our facade of independence to be maintained.

We probably don't even realise we minimise our needs for dependency and support. This includes the importance of relationship in our life, and the softer heart qualities of gentleness, kindness, compassion and love. It may be very difficult for us to show that, like everyone else, we need support, comfort and care. This attitude may also extend to others. So when someone asks us for emotional support, to be comforted or close, we could feel annoyed, angry, or even disgusted by their needs.

In both these scenarios, one part of our wholeness has been inhibited. Consequently, our ability to be inter-dependent is unbalanced. In the first scenario, the balance of dependence and relationship outweighs our need to explore and to be separate and independent. While in the second scenario, our need for the other is quelled in the requirement to be too separate and too independent.

Inter-dependence is a balance of self-reliance and other-reliance. We can ask for our needs from another, as well as be asked by another for theirs. We feel comfortable saying "yes" and "no" to another's wishes, rather than an imbalance of either. We are also able to look after our own needs and assist others to care for some of theirs.

Separate and connected; paradoxically we are both at the same time. We have a clear sense of self apart from the other, as well as a clear sense of relationship with the other. Furthermore, we understand we are an individual/separate person, as well as affect and are affected by each other.

This may seem contradictory, for how can we be both connected and separate? In fact, we cannot be connected unless we are separate, since a relationship is defined by the connection of two separate entities. If we are not separate, there is only *me* or only *you*. If only *I* exist or only *you* exist, there is only one entity and thus no relationship. For a relationship to exist there needs to be an *I* and a *You*, or as Martin Buber puts it, an "I" and a "Thou".[76]

Being Real in Relationships

To engage in I-Thou relationships we need to be centred in our fullness as a human being. If we are estranged from our realness, our heart and soul, we will tend to engage in one sided (I-It) relationships; with ourselves, other humans, other species and the natural environment. Our depleted/false self will take what it wants without understanding our survival, growth and prosperity, depends upon reciprocal connection with that from which it has just taken.

An I-It relationship is also a term coined by Martin Buber. It defines a person who relates to the other as an object for their own needs and gratification.[77] The other or "It" is not seen as a separate person, existing with their own mind, thoughts, feelings and needs.

We may engage in this type of relationship in two ways. We either treat the other person as an "It" or we treat ourselves as an "It". Both these ways of relating could be present in us, although we probably favour one side more than the other. Although they seem quite different, the underlying dynamic is an essential imbalance in inter-dependence and split in the wholeness of self. Let's expand a little on this.

One way we may engage in an I-It relationship is to treat the other person as an "It". Here we relate to the other as an extension of ourselves. We do not acknowledge they have an inner world different and separate from us. So it is possible we sometimes use them to get what we want. To avoid our vulnerability related to inter-dependence, our false self maintains a belief we deserve to get what we want, without thinking about the impact on the other. If the other person does not adhere to our expectations and needs, we will most likely devalue them. The extent of this devaluation will vary; ranging from pointing out, blaming or exaggerating their negative traits, to words and/or acts of dehumanisation. Making the other wrong, allows us to keep our real vulnerability and dependency needs hidden. So the essential nature of our inter-dependence continues to remain out of awareness.

The second way we may engage in an I-It relationship, is by treating ourselves as an "It" and in turn allow the other person to do the same. Here we do not acknowledge our own feelings and needs, but rather focus on what the other feels and needs, so we can adapt to them. As a result, our false self needs the other to fill the emptiness in our lack of wholeness. To maintain this dynamic in relationship, we will tend to exaggerate the positive qualities of the other person, without a balanced appreciation of their limitations. In contrast, we may devalue our self, by being overly aware of our negative attributes and critical of our limitations. In making the other person "so right", we keep our strengths and self-determination hidden. So the essential nature of our inter-dependence, again, remains out of awareness.

In both these I-It relationships, we are unable to engage in reciprocal and balanced relationships. Our false self tends to swing from idealisation and devaluation; of ourselves and the other. Both these ways of being in relationship are not based on a balanced view or awareness that we are essentially inter-dependent, but rather depend upon over-inflating something and then dismissing something else.

There is a middle road to be walked here, where we are aware of our self and the other, in a balanced and reciprocal way. This is what is sometimes referred to as an I-You relationship. In this type of exchange, both people understand they have separate and different personal worlds. That is, each person has their own feelings, desires and needs. Sometimes these will converge with one another, while at other times they will diverge. In addition, there is an understanding that we share a common world, by the mere fact we are both human. This means we will both, for example, have times when we feel sad, angry, surprise, disgust and joy. The subjective experience and nuance of these feelings though, are individual and part of our separate world. Finally, in an I-Thou relationship, as expressed by Martin Buber, we can ultimately acknowledge oneself and the other as an expression of the very essence of "being and aliveness"; of life and the divine.[78]

In I-Thou relationships we are essentially inter-dependent. We are centred in our "being and aliveness", embracing the paradox of connection and separateness. We thus experience times of reciprocity, commonality, agreement, sharing and intimacy (i.e. connection), as well as times of solitude, aloneness, disagreement and difference (i.e. separateness).

Since both people in this type of relationship are whole, there is no need to use each other to *fill* our depleted self or *prop-up* our false self. Consequently, there is no need to over-value ourselves and under-value the other, or under-value- ourselves and over-value the other. In I-Thou relationships, there is room for ALL of us.

In an I-Thou world, there is room for all
cultures, races, religions, genders and species.

Navigating this Path

A word of caution about how we engage in this repair or therapeutic process is prudent here. Repair is always in the service of our *wholeness*. Sometimes when we start this work however, we do it in service of our depleted/false self. For example, we might want to "fix" ourselves, only feel positive emotions, be more perfect, be stronger, be saved, be taken care of, get rid of all our pain, be more lovable or get some desired goal. In this way we strive to be something or to get something, which then continues the avoidance of our wholeness.

If we do this work from our depleted/false self, over the long term, our efforts will be in vain. When we engage in repair work from this perspective, we reinforce the split in our self and continue to negate our "natural being and aliveness". So although we think we are *doing the work*, we are actually moving further away from our wholeness as human beings.

Let's take a simple example. Say we want to reduce our feelings of stress, so we can manage everything we need to do. If we just focus on reducing the stress, without listening to the actual feeling of *stress*, we may reinforce the depleted/false self. We may try and change because we think we shouldn't feel stressed, wonder if there is something wrong with feeling this way, or expect ourselves to accomplish everything without feeling stressed. If however, we begin to listen to this feeling and become curious about what it is telling us and asking of us, we connect more to our wholeness. In this second scenario, we are then more likely to implement change based on our *real* needs.

On the face of it, these two situations may seem only subtly different. In the short-term we may observe very little difference, but in the long term the difference is significant. Change implemented from the perspective of our depleted/false self will probably be short lived. Whereas, change occurring in connection and from the perspective of our "being and aliveness" will have longer term validity.

When we sincerely do this work, the parts of our wholeness which have been rejected, avoided, forgotten or hidden, will arise for us to be seen and included. Basically, when we are authentically navigating this path, the defences of our depleted/false self begin to dissolve, uncovering the wounded (or "shadow") parts of us.

Consequently, there may be many times when we want to avoid the pain and difficulty of this path. This is part of the journey. What we do is our choice. But to progress along this path we are required to allow and embrace all parts of our self, so we may come to embody and know our full humanness.

This can be extremely tricky, as usually these are the parts we don't want to face. So we avoid them, blame others for them, change them or try to get rid of them. It is when we make a conscious choice to embrace these rejected, avoided, forgotten or hidden parts of our self, that we take another step along this path.

Repair in service of our wholeness is about having someone REALLY see us, warts and all, perhaps for the first time in our life.

Doing this work of psychological growth within a relational environment which is supportive, nourishing and genuine, is essential.[79] The three types of relational environment we need to consider include, connection with (1) our "being and aliveness",

(2) other *real* human beings and (3) the natural world around us (i.e. animals, plants, minerals).

One of the reasons we need to do this work within relationship, is that connection is the underlying principle of the circle of life. Everything alive is in relationship to something; allowing it to survive, grow and flourish. For example, a plant only grows in relationship with the earth, sun and rain. This is the same with us; to survive, grow and flourish, we need to be in connection with our "being and aliveness", other human beings and the natural world.

Secondly, we can only develop and grow through "good enough" relationship.[80] So if relationships in our early years were not conducive for our whole self to emerge, and we had to split and adapt our self, we now need to experience relationships which are nourishing and embrace our wholeness. In the loving presence of another, we can slowly let go of our depleted/false self, embrace the pain of our early wounds and begin to touch our "natural being and aliveness"; our fullness as a human being.

This is not a path of recognition, glory, fame, riches or power. Neither are we trying to get somewhere or become someone. It is simply a path of coming home to our heart and soul. My deepest hope is that we will remember our way home.

"I AM DONE WITH GREAT THINGS AND BIG PLANS, GREAT INSTITUTIONS AND BIG SUCCESS. I AM FOR THOSE TINY, INVISIBLE LOVING HUMAN FORCES THAT WORK FROM INDIVIDUAL TO INDIVIDUAL, CREEPING THROUGH THE CRANNIES OF THE WORLD LIKE SO MANY ROOTLETS, OR LIKE CAPILLARY OOZING WATER, WHICH, IF GIVEN TIME, WILL REND THE HARDEST MONUMENTS OF PRIDE."
William James (1842-1910)

Phase Four

A Home

(3-4 years to 6-7 years)

In our building metaphor, we have built the house brick by brick, so we are now ready to include the finishing touches. Here our house becomes our unique *home* in a community of other homes. It is ready to be fully lived in and shared with the various people who will come in and out of our life.

Love, Self-Expression, Sexuality, Competition

I am worthy

I can be both competent and make mistakes | I am centred in
being and aliveness | My world of relationship becomes wider

This fourth phase, starting around three or four years of age until about six or seven, is the final stage in the early development of self. In the previous phases, given a "good enough" relational environment, the infant and toddler has been able to identify and internalise the way their caregivers have assisted to regulate and care for their emotional and relational needs.[81] So now they are more able to do this for themselves.

This "good enough" beginning is essential, for it allows the child in this fourth phase, to go out into the world with a sense of security. So rather than adapting, protecting or negating parts of themselves or parts of others, they can utilise their psychological energy to flourish in the world; through playing, exploring, creating, learning, sharing and loving.

If phase four then continues within a "good enough" relational environment, the child is *on the road* towards mature psychological functioning.[†] Here they are able to experience themselves and others as both complex and whole human beings.

Within this fourth phase, the child has a greater capacity to negotiate separateness in relationships. Cognitively, the child now knows that even though someone might not be physically present, the relationship with that person still exists. For example, a five-year-old knows their mother and the relationship is maintained, even if she goes away for the day. If this child becomes upset, they may be reassured by a phone call to their mother, a memory or substitute object. Since the child can keep the relationship in mind, they can tolerate greater separateness. The child's growing awareness that the other has their own world, also facilitates separation.[82]

[†] I say "on the road", for this is a life-long endeavour which emerges in phase 3, develops more in phase 4 and continues to mature throughout the lifespan.

In addition, the child in this phase has a greater capacity to maintain a stable, yet complex image of relationships.[u] That is, they understand the other person has both good and bad aspects, and although the relationship will sometimes be unsatisfactory, they can see the other is generally okay. Because they can hold ambivalent feelings towards one person (e.g. I both love and hate you), they are also more easily able to tolerate disappointment within the relationship.[83] This developing ability to maintain a stable, yet ambivalent image of another person, allows a child to grow into an adult who is able to sustain long-term relationships.

Given a "good enough" relational environment, the child in this phase also has a greater capacity to sustain a stable, yet complex image of themselves.[v] Here, the child can stand as a separate and unique person. They feel comfortable in their own skin; knowing they are someone with both strengths and weaknesses who is basically okay. They also experience themselves as having a self which is stable and continuous in various situations and relationships. So they don't feel or act as if they are radically different, from one situation to the next or one relationship to the next. This stability allows the child to grow feeling okay about themselves, with a good self-esteem and sense of confidence.

These abilities to experience others and oneself as complex, basically okay and stable over time, are evidence of a budding psychological maturity. This allows the child to grow with the ability to cope with an ever expanding range of relationships and

---

[u] This is called "object constancy", and is part of the theory of Separation-Individuation as formulated by Margaret Mahler. See Appendix for further details about this theory.

[v] This is called "self-constancy", and is part of the theory of Separation-Individuation as formulated by Margaret Mahler. See Appendix for further details about this theory.

experiences, over their life-time.[84] Incorporating a balance of self-assertion and compromise will be their general approach to life and relationships. They will also understand themselves to be valuable and lovable individuals. And because they have a balance of secure attachment and the ability to tolerate separations and disappointments, relationships can be sustained.

A noteworthy aspect of this fourth phase is that the child starts to engage much more with the wider world. As they begin schooling and participate in a larger social community, they interact and build relationships apart from their family. This may include peers, teachers, sport coaches and other families. With this enlarged relational world, the child comes to terms with an expanded reality.

In forming other satisfying attachment relationships, the child can further separate from their primary attachment figures. These new relationships will eventually substitute for their primary attachments. This is particularly evident in adolescence, when an individual's peer relationships begin to take priority over most other relationships. Forming other satisfying connections, apart from one's own family, is a significant developmental milestone for a child. It is important, for it allows them to grow into an adolescent and adult who can form intimate bonds of their own. This then eventually enables them to create their own family[w] and participate as constructive citizens in the wider community.

Through experiencing a wider relational world, a child's sense of self, may be both challenged and expanded. The exposure to social norms, values and relationships, outside their immediate family, may reinforce and/or conflict with what they have

---

[w] Family here is meant in the broadest sense and includes those people we "freely" choose to be in relationship with.

experienced about themselves and relationships in their development so far. For example, at school it is common for a child to learn they need to wait their turn and share the toys. This may present a new challenge for someone who has rarely had to wait or not had to share their belongings with another sibling. Alternatively, a teacher may identify a certain characteristic or strength in a child which has not been recognised in their family. This may allow a positive new experience and growth in the child's identity.

Caregivers will also be impacted by their child's expanding world. As their child separates more, expands their relational world and becomes their own unique person, caregivers may feel challenged and experience ambivalent feelings. This is somewhat similar to the stereotypical and well-known experience of parents who have had children proceed through adolescence. It also occurs in this phase, albeit probably to a lesser degree. Thus, when parents see their child growing into their own personhood (e.g. taking on new values, behaviours and influences), they may experience feelings of both horror and delight in their child's burgeoning growth. As well as managing these ambivalent feelings, caregivers act as facilitators for their child's emergence into the wider world. Here they are required to strike a balance, between, (1) being the wise guide, so their child feels supported in navigating this wider terrain, and (2) letting go of their own ideas and expectations, so their child is free to discover and learn how to navigate this wider terrain in their own unique way.

The child in this fourth phase, grows noticeably in their competence of physical/motor skills, communication/language skills and interpersonal/social skills. A problem which may arise, as a consequence, is that the focus for the child becomes about *achieving* something, at the expense of enjoyment. For example, a child participating in a dance class may be encouraged to become *skilled*, rather than to dance because it is pleasurable. This may be exacerbated as the child begins formal schooling, particularly if the education curriculum is mainly focused around achieving. For example, if they are expected to perform well on tests, rather than to take pleasure in learning.

If achievement is focused on at the expense of enjoyment at this stage, the child may get the message that attaining some goal is more important than what they feel, particularly regarding pleasure and relaxation. Basically, they are learning to *be* by doing, rather than allowing their *doing* to arise from their *being*. This is another version of the false self, where the child has to forgo their "natural being and aliveness", and become something for the environment. In this case, it is to *perform* in a competency or skill.

The child's self-esteem could then become focused around whether they are competent at something or not. If they or others judge themselves as competent, they may feel *good*. But if they or others judge themselves as incompetent, they may feel *bad*.

This child may then have trouble tolerating the anxiety that arises when learning something new. This is potentially problematic, as all new learning includes some anxiety about being a novice and being incompetent. If a child cannot tolerate this anxiety, they will probably try and avoid it. They may do this, for example, by not putting in the required effort when a task becomes challenging. Without perseverance it is difficult to build a new skill. The other way a child may avoid this anxiety, is by becoming so focused on achieving that everything else about the learning process (e.g. enjoyment, pleasure in the moment, aliveness, creativity, integration of meaning, abstraction of learning) gets sidelined. Here the child may become competent at a specific skill, but there is something *deadened* about it. If however, a child can *be with* and tolerate the anxiety of being incompetent, while they learn something new, they will more likely persevere to build the required skill, as well as engage in the moment to moment process of learning. The child's sense of competence here, arises because they have been able to engage fully in the challenge and process of learning, rather than just because they have achieved a particular outcome.

Furthermore, if a child is unable to make mistakes while learning, they may become overly perfectionistic and believe mistakes are "bad". This again can present obstacles to learning, for mistakes are essential in the process of gaining knowledge and skills. Being afraid of making mistakes, means a child will not experiment and test for themselves what works and what doesn't. Curiosity is stifled and true scientific enquiry will be hampered. Furthermore, if a child is anxious about trying something new or doing something different, just in case they make a mistake, their creativity will be smothered. Thus possible new frontiers will probably not be explored.

Emerging Psycho-sexuality

The child in this fourth phase begins to be more conscious of their psycho-sexuality. This includes: Becoming more aware of their biological sex and the sexual differences between male and female. Developing their gender identity through experiencing and expressing the feminine and masculine parts of themselves. And becoming more aware of who they are drawn to and experience feelings of love and attraction towards.

At the most basic level, based on biological sex, a child will usually identify with the same sex and differentiate themselves from the opposite. Biological sex is a term which refers to the chromosomal, hormonal and anatomical characteristics to classify someone as female, male or intersex. This is not to be fused with gender identity, which will be discussed next. Generally, a female child will understand, in terms of biological sex, she is the same as the other females in her life (e.g. mum, sister and girls at school), and different to the males in her life (e.g. dad, brother and boys at school). For a boy it will be the opposite.

Children at this stage become more curious and aware of the physical similarities and differences in body parts (particularly the genitals and breasts) of males and females. For example, they may become more interested in the fact that males have something known as a penis, while females have something different which is called a vagina. They also become more aware of how their physical body is the same or different compared to the significant people in their life. Finally, since a child learns by playing, there may be an increase in their touching and playing with genitalia, allowing them to discover and learn about this part of themselves.

The child, at this stage, also starts to form an identity based upon gender. Gender identity is the internal perception and expression of one's femaleness, maleness, both or other. As mentioned, this is not to be conflated with the identification of biological sex. Many children may identify with the gender which is aligned with their biological sex. For example, I identify with being a girl and I am also biologically a female. Other children however, may identify with the opposite. For example, I identify with being a girl and my biological sex is a male. Or, I identify with being a boy and my biological sex is a female. Still, other children may not identify themselves in a binary way but have a more fluid identification. For example, I identify with being both a girl and a boy, or, I sometimes identify as a girl and at other times I identify as a boy. It is also possible that a child does not identify with gender in these ways, but sees themselves as simply a person, without gender identification.

Identification and differentiation based upon gender, is generally a more complex process than that based on biological sex. This is probably because it is a subjective experience, heavily influenced by the socio-cultural constructions of gender one may draw upon to understand and express this part of themselves. Furthermore, gender identity is not necessarily binary, but multifaceted and fluid. Consequently, it can go awry in numerous ways.

The most notable way the formation of gender identity can become stuck, in this phase, is when a child is expected to adhere to the gender stereotype of their biological sex. For example, a male child is expected to be masculine, while a female child is expected to be feminine. This expectation may restrict a child's developing gender identity into a norm which is not necessarily inclusive of their whole self. Let's look at some examples of how this may occur.

Let's say, as an example, that a male child identifies with the feminine traits of gentleness, nurturance and empathy. When playing he tends to gravitate to the dolls, dressing them up in different outfits and role-playing different relational scenarios with them. But he has caregivers who believe "boys should be boys". In the parenting of their son, they may promote a masculine stereotype of what a boy "should" be, and thus discourage their son's feminine traits, while encouraging more masculine ones. Furthermore, they may become angry, worried, ashamed or disgusted by their son's preference and pleasure in playing with dolls. As another example, let's say, a girl identifies with the masculine traits of strength, assertiveness and power. She also likes to dress-up in male superhero costumes when she goes out (e.g. as Superman). In this case, perhaps she is reprimanded for being too outspoken and impolite, as it doesn't fit the female gender stereotype of gentleness or "being a lady". Maybe her caregivers try to persuade her to dress so she looks more like a girl. For example, they may buy her female superhero costumes. Or perhaps they tell her she can wear the Superman outfit when at home, but when she goes out in public she must wear a dress.

The child, in both these examples, will experience a conflict between what they feel inside and what the outside world expects of them, largely based upon their biological sex and associated gender stereotypes. The message they receive is, "who you are is wrong". This can be especially painful as the child tries to fit themselves into an external world which conflicts with their true nature.

This conflict related to gender stereotypes, may also occur outside the immediate family. For example, when the child goes to school. A boy who identifies with more feminine traits may be teased for being "weak", "girly" or "a sissy". While a girl who identifies with more masculine traits may be ostracised by the other children for being a "tomboy" or "too aggressive". Furthermore, children who do not fit either gender stereotype (e.g. trans* children) may be thought to be weird or that there is something wrong with them. These experiences with one's peers can be particularly painful, especially when a child is ostracised, rejected, teased or bullied as a result. Children who do not align with mainstream gender stereotypes, are usually already struggling with complex feelings about being different to many of their peers. To then be scorned, teased, rejected or isolated because of this difference, can be deeply wounding, confusing and heartbreaking for these children.

To know whether I am biologically a male or a female is

usually"[x] easy. However, the development of gender identity is multilayered, subtle and more about the subjective experience of the child. It may include identification with both femaleness and maleness, rather than just one or the other in a binary fashion. Furthermore, rather than being fixed, it may flow, change and develop. A problem occurs when we expect a child to act in accordance with the gender stereotype of their biological sex, rather than allowing them to creatively experience and express their unique combination of femaleness, maleness and other. When we (as caregivers, other family members and community members) think this and behave to match this ideology, we play a part in restricting the complexity and wholeness of that child.

With a more complex, multifaceted and fluid idea of how a child may experience and express the feminine and masculine parts of themselves, we allow the wholeness of that child.

A normal part of a child's emerging psycho-sexuality, in this phase, is to feel an instinctual impulse to gravitate towards the people (e.g. caregivers and peers) they feel most *drawn to*. The child undergoes an innocent "falling in love" process. They become vulnerable and fully open-hearted to these people.[85] This is an experience of love which is fully embodied and thus may include bodily (sensual) feelings.

In the traditional idea, it was thought the child gravitates towards the opposite-sex parent. So a boy fell in love with his

---

[x] I say "usually" as some children may be born with a combination of both male and female biological sex characteristics. Intersex is a word used to describe these children.

mother, while a girl fell in love with her father. Although this may be the case for a large portion of children, it isn't necessarily the case for every child. A child may also naturally gravitate towards a same-sex person for this embodied experience of open-hearted love. It is also possible some children are drawn towards both sexes (i.e. male and female persons). Furthermore, it is important to note, the person the child is drawn towards is not limited to just the parents or immediate caregivers. Other significant people in the child's life (e.g. aunt, uncle, step-parent, teacher, close family friend and peers) may also play this role for the child.

So firstly, let's look from the traditional standpoint. Here a female child begins to identify with her mother as being of the same sex, but is instinctually drawn to her father. So although she is biologically like her mother, she is also in competition with her for her father's love. The inherent complication is that the female child is required to separate from her mother, but since she is the same sex, she also needs to identify with her at some level. To separate from her mother, identify with her and be in competition with her, is the tight-rope a female child is stepping along at this stage in her development.

On the other hand, in the traditional idea, a male child identifies with his father, but is instinctually drawn to his mother. So again, although he recognises he is like his father, he is also in competition with him for his mother's love. A slightly different internal conflict occurs for the male child compared to the female. He needs to separate from his mother at this stage, but he is also experiencing a falling in love process with her. To separate, but also to be instinctually pulled towards his mother, may create an internal conflict for the male child.

I want to now give voice to the non-traditional dynamics. That is, when the child is instinctively drawn to the same-sex parent.

The female child will then be in competition with her father, as she falls in love with her mother, whom she identifies with, but must also separate from. The male child on the other hand, will be in competition with his mother, as he falls in love with his father whom he also identifies with. Theoretically, this may result in less internal conflict for the male child, in comparison to the female child. That is, the male child can separate more easily from his mother as he is also in competition with her. In both cases, the complexity of these dynamics will probably depend upon the reactions and attitudes of the relational environment; regarding the child's preference to gravitate towards the same-sex person.

This psycho-sexual developmental process, for the child, becomes even more complex when we factor in the type of family unit the child is part of. Traditionally this unit involves a mother and a father. However, in reality it may involve various other caregiver combinations. For example, a single parent, where either the mother or father is physically and/or emotionally absent. It may include a blended family with step-parents and step-siblings. It may also involve same-sex parents or other non-traditional caregiver combinations. In addition, whether the child has other people they can gravitate towards and identify with, such as extended family members or other significant people, will also impact the navigation of this developmental process.

Within this process the child is learning that their natural and open-hearted feelings of love can be held and embraced. They are also beginning to understand they are not included in all relationships. For example, their parents have a "adult" relationship which they are not part of; such as adult conversation, decision making, time alone together and intimacy. Basically, the child is starting to become aware that their caregivers, who up to this point have usually been central to the child's world, have a life of their own. Here, the child comes to terms with the reality that they are not the only one who is having a relationship with this person. This competition for the caregiver's love may bring feelings of aggression and jealousy to the forefront. Consequently, the child at this stage needs to be assisted in managing the emotions of love and open-heartedness on one hand, with feelings of rivalry, aggression and jealousy on the other.

The major problems which can occur, in this innocent "falling in love" process, are if the child's vulnerable open-hearted feelings are (1) rejected, shamed and/or (2) used for the other's self-gratification. For example, a child may express their open-hearted love, to a caregiver by saying, "I love you so much" and perhaps kissing them. If the caregiver feels uncomfortable or maybe even disgusted with such expressiveness, they may ignore the child, push them away, tease them or tell them their behaviour is inappropriate. Alternatively, the caregiver may exploit this innocent openness, by requiring the child to fill a need in them or to act as a substitute for adult intimacy. This may play out in an emotional and/or a more sexual way. For example, a caregiver may want the child to fill an emotional void which exists in their adult relationships, so they use them to satisfy their own needs for love and closeness. Similarly, a caregiver may begin sexualising the relationship they have with the child. This sexualisation may range in degree of severity, from sexually-laced comments to sexual grooming for sexual abuse.

It is also possible the child experiences both (1) rejection/shame and (2) exploitation. In this instance, one caregiver may emotionally/sexually exploit the child, while the other rejects or shames their open-hearted love. Alternatively, the same caregiver may at times emotionally/sexually exploit the child and then at other times reject/shame them.

The consequence for the child, if they are rejected/shamed, will be to reject or feel ashamed of their more primal natures. They may believe they shouldn't have natural human sexual feelings and desires for love. This can lead to a legacy of inner conflict when these feelings and desires arise again, particularly within adult intimate/sexual relationships.

The child, who has been emotionally and/or sexually exploited, may as an adult, feel a deep sense of confusion and betrayal. The significant people in their life, who they thought they could trust and depend upon, have instead taken advantage of them. Consequently, they may have feelings of deep shame, anger and disgust about being *used* for the self-gratification of the other. Complex feelings about their natural impulses, desires and sexuality may also arise. This can result in a legacy of intense inner and outer turmoil. Their sense of self may be filled with conflicted emotions. Their relationship to others, especially when the connection is similar to the type of trusted figure whom they were exploited by, may also be filled with conflicting emotions. Again, this turmoil will probably occur most distinctly, when as an adult, they are engaged in emotionally and/or sexually intimate relationships.

The Legacy
In a "good enough" relational environment, in this fourth phase, our worth is based on who we are, rather than on what we do (or don't do). As we venture out into the wider world, we most likely suffer some disappointment and frustration, and realise the world doesn't revolve around us. During this time, we also begin to get more in touch with our emerging psycho-sexuality, including the expression of our multifaceted gender identity. We learn that the people we love have relationships apart from us; bringing love, aggression and competition to the forefront. If then, our feelings

about these experiences are handled by the significant people in our environment, in an attuned, understanding and mature manner, we will generally have a smooth transition through this phase.

If this was the case for us, we will now feel a healthy sense of worth about ourselves, as well as understand that everyone else is worthy too. We can maintain long-term relationships and find an easier balance of co-operation and competition in these connections. Finally, our sexually intimate relationships are more likely to be based in reciprocal emotional giving.

On the other hand, if our experiences during this time in our life were not attuned to in a "good enough" way, then our legacy may be quite different. Firstly, we may question our fundamental worth. One way we might try to prove our worth to ourselves and others, is through our achievements. Thus, we could be unbalanced in regard to achievement versus enjoyment/relaxation. We may also *do* something in order to *be* someone. Secondly, we might be uncomfortable with more primal feelings such as anger, desire, jealousy, rivalry, greed and disgust. Perhaps we protect ourselves from experiencing these emotions by being somewhat rigid or ordered. Alternatively, we may disconnect or keep on the surface of our feelings, by being busy, chaotic and dramatic. Finally, if our experience of our emerging psycho-sexuality felt rejected, shamed or exploited, we may experience some disconnect between our emotions (i.e. heart) and sex, and thus experience some complications in our adult intimate relationships.

What This Means for Us...Now

If we do not feel fundamentally worthy, just being who we are, then we may have some unfinished psychological business to attend to. We may currently fill this gap through achieving, working hard or trying to be recognised in some way. Perhaps we have difficulty being with the more "messy" emotions of our human experience, and have conflict around the themes of achievement/enjoyment and being/doing. We may also have difficulty integrating emotional connection with our sexuality in our intimate relationships.

Our road to repair begins with allowing ourselves to live from our "natural being and aliveness". Who we are and what we do, arises from this centre in us. It is here we realise our inherent worthiness. So we become more comfortable with allowing ourselves to relax and enjoy the pleasures of life. We will need to become more familiar with this way of *being,* slowly letting go of defining ourselves by our *doing.* It will also be important for us to connect to some of our more primal emotions. We begin to understand feelings such as anger, desire, jealousy, greed and disgust, are simply part of the human experience, as is competition and co-operation within our relationships. In our intimate/sexual relationships, we may need to explore whether we can fully open our heart and enjoy sexual pleasure, or whether we have some difficulty and fears around emotional connection and sex. And finally, in walking this path of psychological growth, we become the "good enough" mother and the "good enough" father for ourselves (and others).

Being Worthy

In this phase of development (3-4 to 6-7 years old), we grow more competent in our physical and emotional/mental capacities and are able to communicate in more complex ways. Although these increasing abilities allow us to become greater participants in the world around us, sometimes the love and attention given by our caregivers is re-directed to focus on these achievements and competencies. Our caregivers do not do this in isolation however, for as we interact more with the outer world, we are immersed in a culture which identifies worth with *doing*, rather than *being*.

If we were assisted to move through this phase in a "good enough" way, we have an embodied *knowing*, "I am good enough". We understand we are worthy for just *being* who we are, rather than having to prove our worth by *doing* something (e.g. achieving, being skilled, getting recognition, being competent).

If this was not the case for us however, as adults we probably base our worth on what we *do*. Doing may become the source of our self-esteem, to such an extent, that we conflate what we do with who we are. In the worst-case scenario, we must *do* something to *be* someone.

If we base our worth on what we *do*, then work probably takes priority in our life. We feel good when we have achieved something and have been productive. Whether this is in our paid work, sports, creativity, parenting or keeping house; achievement is important for us to feel okay about our self. Since productivity and worthiness go hand-in-hand for us, even if we become stressed or tired, we may continue to push ourselves.

If we believe our worth is based upon achievement and

productivity, it will be difficult to give these up. We might become addicted to being busy, achieving, getting recognition and always doing; for the voice inside our head worryingly thinks, "I am only worthy when I do something, so I must keep going".

We may then have difficulty relaxing and enjoying the pleasures of life. Perhaps our social life and relationships are secondary to our work. We might be quite hard on ourselves when we want to rest, perhaps thinking we are lazy or "should" be doing something. The only time we may feel okay to rest is when we become sick or are injured in some way, so we are forced to take a break from our hectic demands. The only other time we can relax is when we are on holiday; here we have an excuse to rest as this is what is "done" on holidays after all.

We may sometimes think people who are less driven to *do* are lazy, selfish or inadequate. Maybe we feel harsh or angry towards them, or believe that at least we are doing the "right" thing, unlike them. It is likely a part of us is angry at our own harsh treatment of our self, continuously pushing to prove we are worthy and okay.

It would be beneficial for us to add a little more play, pleasure, rest and relaxation into our life. Although we'll probably think this suggestion is frivolous. Even though we would love to play and relax more, it is difficult for us to contemplate such an idea. Because with everything we must do, we think we don't have the time.

Is work more important than play?
Is achievement more important than pleasure?

Being then Doing

"Being" is about feeling genuinely alive inside. Donald Winnicott thought that the capacity of *being* is fostered in childhood, through play. When people play together, they feel real, spontaneous and alive.[86] In adulthood, this means engaging in creative arts, sports, pleasurable activities and hobbies, humour and meaningful conversations. It also means not taking ourselves so seriously, having fun and discovering enjoyment with others.

In *being mode*, we are in the moment, non-striving and accepting of our experience. This mode is probably aligned with our right-brain implicit self. This is the part of us which is non-verbal, emotional, inter-connected, intuitive, symbolic, holistic and not able to be fully grasped.[87] In comparison, when we are in *doing mode*, we are achieving, seeking, wanting and acquiring. This is more aligned with our left-brain explicit self, which actively makes sense of things, reflects and communicates.

Why is this important? Well, neuroscience informs us that our right-brain implicit self is the first to develop.[88] Furthermore, this part of us is dominant in our human existence.[89] Therefore, although the left-brain explicit self is more observable, as it is the one which (literally) speaks, we are fundamentally right-brained *beings* first.

Artists, poets, writers, mystics and contemplatives, for millennium, have understood this fundamental truth about us. However, our mainstream culture seems to emphasise the opposite; the *doing* left-brain self. I think it would be true to say that the majority of us have learnt to give more importance to; doing rather than being, thinking rather than feeling, logic rather than intuition, objectivity rather than subjectivity, the verbal rather than the non-verbal.

We are "beings" first.

Recently in mainstream culture, we have seen a growing recognition of the importance of our *being* qualities. For example, the mindfulness movement and a greater interest in our business world on creativity, sustainability and innovation. Even in these instances however, we use *being* to serve our *doing*. That is, for example, we practice mindfulness to perform better, to be more productive, cope with our busy lifestyle or to stop feeling painful emotions. Or we encourage creativity in work, so we can get an edge in the business world and make more money.

I am encouraging something different here; a revolution of sorts. Rather than our *being* qualities in service of our *doing*, I am suggesting our *doing* is in service of our *being*. That is, all our actions arise simply as an expression of our "natural being and aliveness".

We create. We allow intuition to guide us. We live inter-connected to all species. We communicate from our heart and soul. We allow space in our life for uncertainty and the unknown.

Why do we do these things? Simply because they are an expression of who we fundamentally are as human beings.

When we are in touch with our "natural being and aliveness", our doing becomes a creative and spontaneous act.

To deeply understand this *doing arising from being*, in an embodied way, we firstly need to experience just *being* without *doing* something. We stay in *being mode*, until we feel an unmistakable calmness and aliveness throughout our body. Rather than acting on a pre-determined idea or on our urges and desires which are filled with anxiety and fear, we wait and feel for this embodied calmness and aliveness. From here, action arises.

Our *doing* then emerges from our core. Embodied and centred in our "being and aliveness", it expresses our fundamental humanity. That is the difference.

This can be tricky. It requires us to "turn the tables" on our approach to everything we have done and maybe thought was of value about us.

We might feel anxious and want to argue, "But if I let myself be and don't push myself to...exercise, for example, I will end up a sloth and unhealthy. I need to make sure I exercise, right?" The point is, (to continue with this *exercise* example,) when we are truly in touch with our "being and aliveness", we do exercise. Not because we push ourselves and think this is what we "should" do, but because we are in tune with our aliveness and physicality. Since our body expresses itself through movement and action, it wants to dance, run, jump, walk and swim. It wants to sometimes run so fast we can hardly catch our breath. It wants to feel the rush of exhilaration as we dive into the crystal blue ocean water. It wants to sometimes feel the strength of its muscles when we do a push-up. It wants to feel the flow and flexibility when we unwind the tightness in our ligaments, by stretching out slowly and completely. Our body wants to feel the calmness throughout its entire being, when we are still and breathe deeply. Through *being* first, we can tune into what our body needs at any time. Sometimes it needs something vigorous and energetic, while at other times it needs something gentle and relaxing.

In "being" first, what we need to "do"
becomes self-evident.

We can allow room for the anxiety we might feel about *being* first. We may also need to safeguard ourselves against our own and others' expectations of what we "should" be doing. When we stop our habitual tendency to do, the critical voice inside of us may suddenly become quite loud. In addition, if we have always based our worth on what we do, then it is more than likely that others will also have a similar expectation of us, so they might be puzzled and perhaps also a little critical of our change.

Over time we may stop racing around trying to prove our worth with what we do. We become okay with relaxing more into our *being*. So rather than achievement and productivity being our main goal, we begin to value our presence, aliveness, playfulness, interconnectedness, emotions, creativity, intuition and sense of fun. And finally, we breathe easy, relaxing into our full human beingness.[y]

"IT WAS ONLY WHEN I WAS ACTIVELY PASSIVE,
AND CONTENT TO WAIT AND WATCH,
THAT I REALLY KNEW WHAT I WANTED."
Marion Milner (1934) In, *A Life of One's Own*

---

[y] See box on the following page titled "Something to Experience".

Something to Experience

When ready, take a few relaxed breaths...focusing on the breath coming in and out of the body.....After a few moments, perhaps take a few more breaths, allowing yourself to be fully present here, just breathing in and out...

Notice what it is like to stay here for a few moments. Do you begin to feel restless, agitated, scared, uncertain, stupid...is it also possible you touch a feeling of calm, relaxation or aliveness?

There is no need to manufacture an experience, for there is no right or wrong way to feel. Just notice how your experience unfolds, whatever that may be. You are also not trying to get somewhere or do something; but are simply breathing and *being with* your experience right now.

Rest here for as long as you like...

Experiencing "Messy" Emotions

If we have become stuck at this phase in our development, we may now as an adult avoid our more primal feelings. Depending upon our individual circumstances in this phase of growth, we may do this in one of two ways. Perhaps we overly control our feelings, through adherence to certain rules, ideas or principles. Alternatively, we may remain on the surface of our feelings, by exaggerating or dramatising what we experience. In both positions, we are not consciously in touch with the depth of our emotions.

In the first instance, we may think it is important to control our more primal feelings. Perhaps we learnt it is *not acceptable* to express certain emotions. So now, rather than act with our affective nature, we might repress our feelings and think we need to do the "right" thing and behave in an "ideal" way. We might, for example, act from an idea of duty, obligation or responsibility, even when our deeper feelings are suggesting something different.

Experiencing feelings such as anger, greed, desire, disgust, envy and jealousy, can be filled with conflict for us. Quite possibly, we find it difficult to admit to and connect to some of these feelings. We may even pride ourselves on being able to stay above this sort of human messiness. So when such "messy" emotions seep through the cracks of our control, we probably criticise ourselves severely.

Maybe we were, and possibly still are, part of a family or social group adhering to a particular moral code; so we behave according to certain rules. This is most obvious within religious families and communities. It may also occur in other ways, such as with guidelines related to politeness, social conventions and social status expectations. These moral codes and principles give us guidelines on how to behave and live; enabling us to quickly assess what is "right" and what is "wrong". However, when we adhere to these codes, without consideration of our moment-to-moment subjective experience, our behaviour can become rigid and sterile. For example, if we have been conditioned to smile politely when someone says hello and asks how we are, we may abide by this code of conduct, even if sometimes a part of us wants to respond differently.

Our thinking style also may be a little black and white. So we mightn't understand the shades of grey other people are okay to live with. In addition, when others do not abide by what we think is "right", we can become indignant, finding it difficult to understand how they cannot see the "wrongness" in their ways. We might secretly think, "if everyone did the right thing (or aligned themselves with higher principles), the world would be a much better place".

Finally, we may live within structured routines and be quite orderly in the way we function. Although this may be beneficial and adaptive in many areas of our life, it could restrict our full human beingness. That is, it may obstruct our natural, spontaneous, creative and alive nature.

Alternatively, we may hover above our deeper emotions by amplifying or dramatising our experience. In this way, we distract ourselves and other people from what we *really* feel.

Even though we might come across to others as highly impassioned, since our style of expression is quite theatrical, our authentic emotional expression is lost. Being dramatic is entertaining and a kind of performance, which then means we can remain on the surface of our experience.

This strategy acts as a smokescreen, allowing us to keep out overwhelming and powerful emotions. It also keeps others away from our *realness*, and thus keeps us safe from being hurt, overpowered or exploited by them.

Another way we distance ourselves from our emotions, is to live a life which is chaotic or disorganised. Perhaps we fill our days with many things to do, do not organise ourselves effectively and/or tend towards having mini dramas. We believe we are genuinely busy and have a lot to do, thus rationalising our chaos and disorganisation. Although we do seem to have more than our fair share of life to contend with, there is usually an ulterior reason we jam pack our days and run from one thing to the next. How can we *really* feel what is going on in our internal world, when "so" much happens to us and we are "so" busy?

This strategy of staying on the surface of our emotional experience, has a cost; to ourselves and our relationships. Drama and chaos can be overwhelming and so we may become tired, stressed or physically ill living such a *hectic* life. We can also miss out on being taken seriously by other people. This is a little like the fable *The Boy Who Cried Wolf*. In this story, a shepherd boy cries for help as if he has seen a wolf. The villagers run to assist him, only to find there is no wolf. This happens again. Soon after, the shepherd boy does see a wolf. Unable to protect the sheep on his own, he desperately cries for help. The villagers, tired of his game, do not come and the sheep are mauled. In all the drama of our life, other people sometimes take our concerns less seriously. Despite caring for people, our tendency for chaos and dramatisation may anger, overwhelm or distance them. This can lead to problems within some of our more intimate relationships.

It is not that we don't feel deeply; we do. The problem is we feel overpowered by these emotions. Alternatively, we may worry about showing our *realness*; expecting to be rejected, exploited or overpowered by the other person. So, it could be particularly wounding for us when people don't take us seriously. Paradoxically, it would be reparative for us to touch and allow someone else to see the depths of our emotional inner world.

Even though these two positions seem worlds apart and polar opposites, they are hiding a similar dynamic. That is, we think the "messiness" of our internal world is "unsavoury" and that some of our more primal feelings are "bad". As such, we have learnt to either control these parts of us or deflect away from them with a smokescreen of drama and chaos.

On this path to becoming fully human, we understand our "messy" emotional world is an important part of who we and others are. Our wholeness includes both shadow and light. Without the play of these opposites, we are merely one-dimensional; more like a cardboard cut-out than a full human being.

~ ♥ ~

Balancing the Feminine and Masculine

Sometimes in this phase, we may become polarised in regard to our ideas around the feminine and the masculine. We could have stereotyped views of what a male should be (e.g. strong, powerful, self-assured) and what a female should be (e.g. gentle, submissive, nurturing). Within each person however, there is a mix of both feminine and masculine traits and/or energy. This is different to the biological sex of a person.

At times we may feel our femaleness
At other times we may feel our maleness
Sometimes we may feel both
And from time-to-time we may feel neither

Borrowing from Taoist Chinese philosophy, feminine relates to yin and masculine to yang. These are simply opposite aspects which make up the whole. In this philosophy, everything exists in relation to its opposite, so we cannot have one without the other. For example, we cannot have day without night or light without dark. In addition, there is recognition within this philosophy that there is always a bit of the opposite in something. This is illustrated in the well-known yin/yang symbol, where a circle is divided into dark and light; there is a bit of light in the dark side and a bit of dark in the light side.

Each of us then, has a mixture of both feminine (yin) and masculine (yang) traits. Feminine traits may include; intuitiveness, receptivity, empathy, flow, sensuality, nurturing, affection, sharing and patience. Masculine traits may include; logic, focus, integrity, stability, passion, independence, discipline, confidence, and strength. Our socialisation may affect how we personally experience and express these traits. Ultimately though, our wholeness includes a balance of both.

If we are lopsided in this balance of feminine and masculine, the traits we display will be compromised. So firstly, when there isn't a balance of the masculine within the feminine, the following may occur: Without some grounding in reality, our *intuition* becomes delusion. Without discernment, our *receptiveness* becomes overwhelm. Without wisdom, our *empathy* is ineffectual. Without structure, our *flow* cannot be utilised. Without restraint, our *sensuality* becomes desire we cannot satisfy. Without limitations, our *nurturing* becomes indulgence. Without hate, our *love* is sickly sweet. Without some self-interest, our *sharing* becomes impoverishment. Without purpose, our *patience* becomes complacency.

On the other side, without the balance of the feminine within the masculine, the following may occur: Without emotion, our *logic* becomes irrelevant. Without heart, our *focus* becomes barren. Without kindness, our *integrity* becomes self-righteousness. Without spontaneity, our *stability* becomes restrictive. Without receptiveness, our *passion* becomes aggression. Without community, our *independence* becomes isolation. Without freedom, our *discipline* becomes oppressive. Without humility, our *confidence* becomes arrogance. Without flexibility, our *strength* becomes brittle.

Our wholeness calls us to embrace both the feminine and masculine. This can be a hard-won balance and something we may be challenged with throughout our life.

How can I add a little yin to my yang?
How can I add a little yang to my yin?

Sometimes the conflicts in our life will involve this theme of feminine and masculine imbalance. For example, one part of us wants something, but rather than actively taking steps towards trying to achieve it, we wait passively and magically hope something will occur. This is an imbalance of the feminine without the masculine. This is like someone who has a piece of land and dreams of planting and harvesting a crop, but never actually does it. Alternatively, we might be someone who has a tendency towards constant action, without the balance of passivity. So rather than trusting and having patience, we continue to take action when it is not effective. This shows too much masculine without the necessary balance of the feminine. This would be like someone who having planted their crop, becomes impatient, rips it up before it is ripe and puts another crop in its place.

Feminine and masculine imbalances also occur between people and within relationships. For example, one person in the relationship may be more disciplined and rigid, while the other is more carefree and chaotic. In an attempt to become more whole, we may be drawn to people who express our opposite. Here we have a reparative opportunity; to get in touch with a part of our self we are not so aware of.

Often however, these feminine and masculine imbalances, within our relationships, become a battle ground. Let's look at an example of this. While on holiday, one person likes to plan everything they do, while the other prefers waking up each day and being spontaneous. These opposing feminine and masculine traits, may have created the initial attraction to one another; "I find in you the wholeness I disown in myself". The person who plans everything, may be attracted to the feeling of freedom their more carefree and spontaneous partner provides them. While their planning and routine provides the spontaneous partner with some sense of stability and security. We can also imagine however, the potential for conflict which could occur when these two people go on a holiday together.

To navigate the opposing forces we discover within our self is tricky enough. To then navigate the opposing forces between our self and the self of the other, in relationship, is more complex and may sometimes feel excruciatingly difficult.

~ ♥ ~

Navigating Competition and Co-operation

In our experience of living, we navigate a vast array of competing phenomena; within our self and then between our self and others. The challenge to maintain the integrity and needs of one self and the act of being with the integrity and needs of the other, is a life-long endeavour. This contest, between what *I am* and want and what *You* are and want, is a tricky tightrope to walk. How we balance the *I* and *You*, will probably determine whether we fall into conflict or attain harmony. This is a very human struggle.

It makes sense that when our goals, for example, are similar, we can co-operate more easily. When our goals are different, competition begins. This is clear in team sports, where one group has the same goal and thus work together, against another group who have a different goal.

In team sports, the rules and goals of the game are made explicit, and so play within certain boundaries is possible. In our personal relationships however, the rules and goals are not always explicitly stated. Furthermore, our personal interactions will sometimes involve similar goals, like we are playing on the same team, and sometimes different goals, as if we are on opposing teams. As a result, our personal play (or interactions) can become complex, confusing and somewhat tricky to navigate.

Here's an example. One person goes into a business partnership with the explicit goal of making money, but also wants to be recognised, prove their worth and be admired. The other person goes into this business partnership with the same explicit goal of making money, but also wants to have an adventure which is enjoyable, fun and not too much commitment. These business partners are probably aware of their comparable goal of wanting to make money. However, they may be less aware of their other goals, which will inevitably impact how each approaches the daily tasks of running the business, solving problems and making decisions. At times they will align and thus be able to co-operate quite easily. While at other times they won't, and will be required to negotiate their competing (and often unspoken) needs; without a rule book to guide them or an umpire to mediate their play.

The struggle of being with our own self, while being with how we have construed the other, as well as the experience of our be-tween-ness, emerges with our every encounter in the world.[90] Thus, within all our relationships, we will probably experience some struggle between co-operation and competition.

Perhaps in a way, we come to terms with the fact that each person is at the centre of their own world, and that we are here to share the human experience.

Sex and Emotional Connection

During this fourth phase our developing psycho-sexuality becomes more evident. The way our relational environment relates to this part of us, may impact the way we engage in sexually intimate relationships as an adult. In general, wholeness in our sexual intimacy is an experience which includes both our physicality (i.e. body, genital area, pelvis) and our being and aliveness (or heart and soul). This means our physical act of sexual intimacy occurs with emotional connection; with our self and the other.

If the significant people in our life accepted, recognised and cherished the expression of the diversity in this part of our self, then our experience of sexual intimacy as an adult may feel satisfying. We can probably express our sexuality and heart-felt feelings without shame or censor. Being able to speak about our sexual and emotional intimate needs quite openly, we can also discuss any problems which may arise in this area of our life.

If however, during this stage of development, the significant people in our life rejected, shamed and/or exploited our developing sexuality, then our experience with sexual intimacy may be more difficult. To protect ourselves from further rejection, shame or exploitation, we may sever the connection between our sexual behaviour and heart-felt feelings. Here we experience a disconnect between the physical act of sex (body/pelvis) and our emotions (heart and soul).

For some of us, our sexual intimacy may just include our body/pelvis, without much heart and soul. Here we can experience and gain sexual pleasure and enjoyment, but we do not allow ourselves to be emotionally connected. Perhaps without being aware, we distance our emotional self when engaging in sex. Including our heart and soul, with the person we are having sex with, might mean we feel emotionally vulnerable and more exposed to getting hurt, being rejected or exploited.

On the other hand, some of us may include our heart and soul, but exclude our body/pelvis. In this case, we can feel emotionally close to someone, but find it difficult to experience and express our full sexual aliveness. We may thus inhibit our full sexual desire, pleasure and enjoyment. Maybe we fear this part of our self, or fear the other person's reaction to our full sexual nature.

Others of us may manage this disconnect by enjoying sexual pleasure with one person, while being emotionally connected with another. So we might experience an emotional connection with one person, but our feelings of sexual desire for them are dampened down. Then with another person, we can experience sexual desire and pleasure, but the emotional connection with them is somewhat lacking. Here, we have difficulty including both sex and emotional connection within the one relationship.

There are many forms of sexual intimacy in the world today, so it can be difficult to discern what constitutes a disconnect in our wholeness. I want to propose an idea, which includes two factors. If we do not have both factors in our sexual intimacy, then it is possible we are disconnected in this part of our self and perhaps have some unfinished psychological business to attend to.

The first of these factors is: when we engage in any sexual behaviour, it is an act of emotional giving.[91] A good test, to check if this has occurred, is whether the recipient of our sexual-emotional giving (if asked) experiences it as such. This test stops self-deception, where we may surmise, "Of course my sexual intimacy is filled with emotional giving". If the other person doesn't experience it as such, then perhaps we have cause to question whether it is so. Alternatively, we may believe that the other person cannot "receive" our (sexual) emotional giving. This is a possibility too. If this is what we assume is occurring, we would ask the other to assist us to understand what is happening emotionally for them. In this situation, we would then become more aware of what they need to be able to take in our sexual emotional giving.

The second factor is: when we engage in any sexual behaviour, we can take in the emotional giving of the other. That is, within the sexual act, our heart and soul is open to receive the other.

Essentially then, wholeness in sexual intimacy is a reciprocal act of emotional giving. We both give and we both receive. It includes our full being and aliveness (body/pelvis, heart and soul) in connection with the other person's full being and aliveness (body/pelvis, heart and soul). Without this connection, our sexual activity could become more aligned with a physical workout, a performance, masturbatory self-gratification, a stop gap for loneliness or an expulsion of aggression. In more extreme cases of disconnection, it may also become assault, exploitation or abuse. To be clear, this two-factor proposal, of whether our sexual intimacy is whole or split, is not based on our sexual preference (i.e. the type of sexual intercourse, stimulation or gratification we like to receive and participate in). Neither is it based on our sexual orientation (that is whether we are heterosexual, gay, lesbian, bisexual, asexual or another diverse sexual orientation).

Wholeness in sexual intimacy is a dance of giving and receiving; a flow of physical and emotional intimacy.

The "Good Enough" Mother and Father

Through a "good enough" relationship, we can take in the nurturing, nourishment, wisdom and strength we require to grow, mature and flourish. In this way, over time and throughout our life, we become the "good enough" mother and the "good enough" father for ourselves and others.

When we are in touch with the "good enough" mother, we take care of our needs and nourish our self. We understand creating is the natural expression of our "being and aliveness". We engage in reciprocal relationships, where both people are seen, heard and cared about. This understanding is extended to all species (i.e. plants, animals and minerals); for our heart knows we are all connected, inter-dependent and vital expressions of life.

In contrast, when we are in touch with the "not good enough" mother, we may become self-critical and impatient. Perhaps we strive for perfection and judge ourselves according to some standard arbitrarily chosen. We may direct anger and hate towards ourselves and perhaps blame our self (or another) for our situation. We may also gravitate towards relationships which are loveless, empty, artificial, or destructive. We could become so focused on the other person and what they need, we forget our self and what we need. It is possible we even sacrifice an important part of our self, for the familiarity of relationship; for we fear being alone.

When we are in touch with the "good enough" father, we gain clarity about what is important to us. We proactively work towards what is meaningful and protect ourselves from influences that may sabotage our efforts. We have the strength, stamina and commitment to work through the struggles and problems which will undoubtedly arise. We are willing to face up to the shadow parts of our self, particularly our self-centeredness, which may have a negative impact on us and others. We actively pursue the knowledge our heart deeply desires, and bravely step into the unknown and the unexplored. Finally, for the benefit of all beings, we have the courage to speak our truth, even when it is inconvenient.

On the other hand, when we are in touch with the "not good enough" father, we overvalue the material world and objectivity, while dismissing the immaterial world and subjectivity. Perhaps we treat ourselves and others like a resource to be used and abused, without understanding the consequences of our disconnection and objectification. We do not question our actions and wonder about the impact they have, nor do we bring a curious attitude to our habitual patterns. In our quest for knowledge and wisdom, we may dip our investigative toe in to satisfy our curiosity; but we stop too short, and so don't acquire real clarity or true wisdom. Possibly we fear what we'll find. Because if we really looked deeply, we would have to revolutionise the way we think about ourselves, others and the world we live in.

She understands she is creation; life itself.
She is lived by this mystery.

He understands, creation requires an agent
to bring something into existence.
Self-centredness obstructs this process.

The Potential of this Path

At this phase, our foundation and house are solid enough to stand a complete renovation (or revolution) in the way we see, understand and experience life. We thus have the potential here, to fully engage in the paradox and complexity of our humanity; and over time see beyond the dualistic concepts most of us habitually get stuck in. My hope then for those of us on this path, is that we embrace and playfully explore this becoming fully human.

"OUT BEYOND IDEAS OF WRONGDOING AND RIGHTDOING THERE IS A FIELD. I'LL MEET YOU THERE. WHEN THE SOUL LIES DOWN IN THAT GRASS THE WORLD IS TOO FULL TO TALK ABOUT."
Rumi, translation by Coleman Barks

PART III

On this path of psychological healing, growth and becoming whole, we have three guides to assist us. They include; emotion, relationship and time. Although others could be included, these are probably the major guiding principles which underlie this psychological work. Knowing and heeding these will assist our journey.

Guide 1: Emotion

On this journey, we will meet the body-based emotions which have been kept unconscious. These are the parts of our wholeness which we needed to negate, to adapt and survive the failures of our relational environment. To become whole, these are the parts we need to re-discover and embody into our conscious sense of self.

Emotional Regulation versus Avoidance

Given the right trigger, the negated emotional parts held in our un-conscious can suddenly come alive in us. Our emotional reaction to the present situation, at these times, can take on a life of its own; surprising both ourselves and other people. Perhaps we become overwhelmed (e.g. via rage, anger, disgust, fear) or underwhelmed (e.g. via disassociation, shame, numbing, cutting off). We could also experience both in succession; feeling like a "whirlpool" or "rollercoaster" as we cycle through overwhelming and under-whelming emotional states. It is quite likely then, to avoid such occurrences happening too often, we've developed habitual ways to regulate our emotional inner world.

The methods we find to regulate and soothe our emotions can be as varied as life itself. We may draw upon the external world (e.g. alcohol, relationships, work, nature, computers, entertain-ment, external codes of conduct) as well as our internal world (e.g. phantasy, pride, opinions, imagination, memories). The question then arises, what is growth-promoting in these methods of emo-tional regulation and what is not?

Firstly, it is not about the activity inherently, but the way we relate to it and are attempting to use it, which are the most im-portant considerations. For example, we clean our house because we (unconsciously) want to avoid feelings of anxiety or anger. Or we clean our house to nourish ourselves by living in a pleasant en-vironment. In this example, cleaning to avoid feelings is simply compounding the problem, for we are distracting ourselves from an emotion which needs to be felt, seen, heard and embodied. It would be different if say, cleaning our house was an activity which allowed us to regulate the energetic intensity of our emotion, so that afterwards we were able to reflect upon our feelings. If we engage in something for the purpose of avoiding our emotions, even though in the short-term we might feel better, we are not connecting with and including an important part of our whole self.

In addition, if we feel a type of *compulsion* attached to whatever we engage in, we are also probably avoiding a part of our self. For example, I am sometimes driven to gain more knowledge in an attempt to understand my emotional world. This compulsion to intellectually understand something means I remain in my head, rather than feeling and connecting to the emotions in my body. This is similar for those of us who feel a *driven* quality in our eating (whether it is over eating, not eating, healthy eating, unhealthy eating), drinking, drug taking, exercising, working, relationships, sex, love, reading, social media, watching TV, picking at our skin, helping others, talking, cleaning, spending time alone, spiritual practice, socialising, etc. See, it is not the activity per se, but the way we engage in it and use it.[z]

If our activity/behaviour is starting to cause problems in our life, we are more likely to put effort into trying to stop the compulsive or driven aspect of it. Sometimes we are successful and sometimes we are not. Sometimes we are successful because we just change the activity/behaviour we are being compulsive about, so in actuality nothing has changed at all.

We will get much more "bang for our buck" if we put effort into discovering what we are seeking, when we compulsively engage in these activities or behaviours. Usually it's something to do with avoiding painful emotions and wanting to feel better.

To feel better, paradoxically, our pain needs to be felt, heard,

---

[z] See box on the next page titled "How Does My Self-Soothing Weigh Up?"

seen and cared about. This needs to be done in the presence of another and when alone.

So rather than compulsively avoid our internal world, we begin to allow these emotional parts of us to be included in our whole sense of self. We begin to find ways to touch, be with, express and thus regulate our emotional energy. As a result, the activities and behaviours we were compulsively driven to do, will slowly become impotent as their function (of avoiding our internal emotional world) becomes obsolete.

How Does My Self-Soothing Weigh Up?

An exercise: Begin by bringing to mind an activity or behaviour you regularly do. Then as you hold this in mind, ask yourself the following questions:

1. How do I feel as I engage in this activity/behaviour?
2. Does this activity/behaviour allow me to soothe and regulate the intensity of the emotion, so I have the mind space to reflect and come to a better understanding about what triggered the emotion?
3. Do I engage in this activity/behaviour to avoid feeling something?
4. What would I experience and feel if I didn't engage in it?

Through these questions you may get a sense of whether you are engaging in the activity/behaviour as a compulsive way to avoid something, or as a way to regulate your emotional energy, take care of yourself and nourish yourself. How does *your* activity/behaviour weigh up? If some of them are more about avoidance, perhaps you might consider how you can tweak your engagement in that activity/behaviour, so it leans more towards regulating the intensity of the emotion, taking care of yourself and nourishing yourself.

Embodiment of Pain and Pleasure

Allowing space for all parts of our self, the painful and the joyful, is our road to repair. We cannot choose one without the other, as like a coin they are two different faces of our "being and aliveness". Pleasure and pain come as a package deal. In recovering our full humanness, we will excavate both. Some of us think we can have joy without the pain. This is false, as both sides reflect our wholeness. If we want to avoid or numb the pain, our pleasure will also be shunned and deadened. Being with both equally, is the work.

We will probably have many stops and starts on this journey. Often in this type of internal work, the times when we want to stop are the times when we have "hit a wall" of growth. To grow beyond this stuck point, we need to step through the wall to come out the other side. The process of stepping through however, is experienced as unsettling, painful, heavy, unknown, frightening or unusual. Until we step through. Then we experience feelings of expansion, newness, lightness, aliveness and joy.

We cannot skip the "bad" bits to get to the "good" bits. Our mind might try and think of all sorts of ways we could do this however. We probably become very creative with our ideas at this point. But the simple fact is, in this type of psychological growth, the pain is often the grist we require to move through our stuckness and grow.

Painful emotions are telling us something
important. They need to be seen, listened to,
connected with and cared about.

Utilising Painful Emotions to Grow

We might wonder whether it is *really* necessary to work with the painful emotions that arise for us. Why can't we just be whole without all this talk of pain? Why not take a pill? Can't we just non-judgementally let the pain come and go, or leave it in the hands of a Higher Source? And since we can only change in the present, isn't it a waste of time looking at our painful past?

Certainly, some of these ideas are valid. However, they are only truly valid when we have done the *work* of coming in direct contact with all our experience, including our negated painful parts. This work is a process of knowing via embodiment, rather than knowing with our intellect. Without this, the above reasons are merely ways to avoid the *real* work.

It is the same if we want to build a house. We cannot just pop a pill or imagine the great house we want and expect it to appear. Allowing a house to come and go in our mind will not give us shelter from the cold and rain. Believing in a Higher Source is comforting, but it isn't going to lay the first brick. And yes, we need to lay each brick in the present moment. However, if we discover our training as a builder was faulty and we do not know how to build a sturdy house, we will need to do a little re-training, so we can build something that stands strong for a long time.

So just like a builder needs to lay every single brick, one by one, we also need to get our hands dirty. We need to prepare the land, dig the holes, mix up the cement, lay the bricks and bang the nails into the roof. Without our hard work and consistent effort, from dawn to dusk, no house will ever be built, renovated or repaired. Therefore, if we do not do the *necessary work*, our wholeness as human beings will stay in the realm of possibility, rather than ever becoming an actuality. The pain we encounter in our life, is akin to the dirty work we need to trudge through to build a strong and sturdy foundation and house.

To provide more traditional metaphors for this idea; a lotus flower rises from the mud, gold is panned from dirt and an oyster uses the grit to form a pearl. In other words, the painstaking work we do to bring awareness to our negated emotional parts, is like the manure to fertilise our growth. Just like a lotus needs the mud, gold needs the dirt and pearls need the grit; we utilise the pain to grow.

So how do we work with this pain manure, so it acts as a fertiliser for our growth? As a general rule, we need to do the opposite of our habit of avoiding it. Usually we want to do one of the following; steer clear of it, get rid of it, move on from it, analyse it, work it out, disconnect from it, blame someone else for it, distract ourselves from it or ignore it hoping it will go away. Pain will not totally overwhelm us, nor is it bad, ugly, disgusting or wrong. Grief and heartbreak are parts of our experience of being alive, just as joy and pleasure are. So rather than habitually resisting pain and clinging to pleasure, we move towards *opening to* and *being with* whatever arises; inhabiting our full human experience.

Through consciously embodying all our emotional states of being, we evolve a more coherent and secure sense of self.

"Being With" Emotion

Often, we may try and *think* through our emotions, rather than *feel* them through. Emotions though are not just intellectual. They are body-based and hence have a physical nature. For example, when we feel hurt, we might sense a physical pain and wound in our heart area. When nervous we may experience a sensation of butterflies in our stomach, our chest might tighten, we might find it difficult to breathe and our body might feel light or shaky. So we cannot just *think* through our emotions. We need to literally connect, stay with and *feel* them through. Basically, we need to *be with* our emotions, before we can *make sense* of our emotions.

> "A NATURAL HUMAN BEING WOULD BE MORE LIKELY TO START FROM 'I FEEL, THEREFORE I AM'."
> H Guntip (1968). In, *Schizoid Phenomena, Object Relations and the Self.* p, 65

In *being with* emotion, we begin by attuning to and experiencing the physical feelings in our body. This *being with* is imbued with a certain flavour. Kindness, care, gentle strength, presence and acceptance, are all good words to describe this flavour. So we are *feeling with* parts of our self; attending to and allowing space for the freedom of expression of these emotional parts.

This is the tricky bit, as these emotions can feel painful and bad. We want them to stop or to get rid of them. We may become impatient, frustrated, annoyed and overwhelmed. Consequently, we need to draw upon every ounce of our gentle strength and warrior spirit to be patient and present with whatever arises.

In this process, a part of us attends to our self doing this. This part is our awareness or observing self. It is the part which attunes to the process of what we are doing; it discerns the effect and whether we need a little more of something or a little less of something. This is a bit like a mother holding a crying baby in her arms. She is present; without being too distant or too involved. She also observes the impact her soothing attempts have on her baby, adjusting and attuning to what has the best result. Importantly, she is patient, understanding and gentle in her approach.

There is a second aspect in *being with* emotion which we need to consider. That is, taming our habitual thoughts. When we experience an emotion, stories and ideas about what the emotion means can overtake our mind. These stories and ideas may be interesting or give us a way to make sense of what we are feeling, but they are not conducive to *being with* the emotion. In fact, when we pay too much attention to these stories and ideas, they distract us from our emotions. This usually means the emotion is prolonged, we continue with our habitual story and nothing changes.

Basically, with awareness imbued with kindness, we focus directly on feeling into the actual centre of the pain (or pleasure); the raw, physical feeling. We stay with that. If our thinking mind pulls us away, we notice and gently bring our awareness back to the play of emotional energy in our body.

Once we have *felt* through the emotion, we may then, bring in our thinking mind to reflect upon it. Here we may take some time to make sense of it, grapple with what it means for us, problem solve something if necessary and gain some insight.

Although the actual process may not be as clear cut as what I am alluding to here, I want to emphasise the importance of firstly *being with* the raw physical feeling; as real insight only arises from our embodied experience.

The Next Level:
Playing with Emotional Energy

Emotion is energy in motion. This energy is neither inherently positive nor negative. It may seem like one or the other at the time, but if we take a really close look, emotion is simply energy which we then label as good or bad. In fact, if we *really* examine each emotion, we discover both positive and negative physical states. For example, bliss feels both extraordinarily great and extraordinarily painful. It is a little like a sexual orgasm, it feels both pleasurable and painful at the same time.

Like all sources of energy, the energy inherent in our emotions, if harnessed, may be utilised. This is like the energy of the sun or water being harnessed to produce power. This power can then be used for creative or destructive purposes, depending upon the requirement of the situation.

Life is a continuous cycle of creation and destruction. We need both to develop and grow.

In infancy and childhood, given a "good enough" relational environment, we engage in this creation and destruction to facilitate our growth.[92] If however, we did not have such a facilitative environment, these creative and destructive forces probably were not embodied and so as adults we experience them unconsciously. Rather than facilitate our growth, these unconscious forces inhibit our growth. If this is the case, we may intuitively know we have this creative energy and feel its possibility, although have trouble harnessing and directing it and therefore perhaps waste its potential.

We may also experience our destructive energy quite intensely and possibly feel afraid or overwhelmed by it. Again, we are unable to utilise it and so it swamps the life we could potentially create.

Without conscious awareness and embodiment of all parts of us, we remain at the mercy of these emotional forces. Like a rider who hasn't harnessed the energy of a horse, will be thrown to and fro, we are continuously pushed and pulled by our (unconscious) emotional states.

So how do we harness emotional energy? Emotional energy is harnessed by connecting to the physicality, sensation and feeling in our body, while our observing self (or awareness) acts as a vessel or container for this energy. Essentially, our emotions are akin to the sun, our body is the solar panels and our observing self (or awareness) is the grid which converts the sun into the energy that may be utilised.

To do this requires strength of self. This strength means we have a capacity to observe and be aware of what we are experiencing, without getting lost, overwhelmed or detached. If we do not have this strength yet, we may need someone (e.g. therapist) to assist us with building it. This may be the case if we have an insecure or disorganised/disorientated attachment. Individually, we can also build awareness through practicing meditation. With greater strength in our observing self, we will be able to contain and utilise the emotional energy flowing through our body.

Having an attitude of *playfulness*, even though harnessing emotional energy can be tricky work, is beneficial to this process. This playfulness is a bit like that of a young child.

If this child was at the beach, they might begin by getting sand and creating what we adults label as a sand castle. In their creation they do not have a preconceived idea of what a sand castle is or should look like (unless conditioned by us adults). Neither do they stress about how they "should" go about constructing it. They are simply embodied doing what comes naturally. They see sand, they start to dig in it and transfer it to different places. What it looks like at the end is a result of their spontaneous play process. It is not judged as good or bad. They also do not create this form for a certain outcome. Playing is the point!

If the child is still young enough to engage in spontaneous play, they'll eventually stamp on this hump of sand, putting their full energy into destroying what they have just built. This destruction is a natural and important part of their play. For then they have the *space to create* something else. This is how they grow.

Just like the growth occurring in the natural world is underpinned by a continuous cycle of creation and destruction. The child destroys (death) to enable creation (life), which results in a continuous process of play (or growth).

So play! For play is the point.

Guide 2: Relationship

We get the most benefit when we do this psychological repair work within relationship.[aa] It is in the presence of a "good enough" other that we learn to *be with* our whole self, including painful emotions.

It is the *felt* experience of someone else seeing, tolerating, accepting, understanding and caring about ALL of us, which enables us to do the same for ourselves. It is also in seeing and experiencing another person connect to their own emotional world that we understand how we may relate to ours. Within this relational experience we don't have to ignore, reject or hide parts of our self. We can *be with* our whole self; both with others and when alone.

[aa] Throughout this section when I refer to relationship, I am assuming it is "good enough".

Wholeness through Relationship

One of the quickest routes, on the road to becoming whole, is to recognise our (unconscious) negated parts in the experiences we have in relationship. Those closest to us, such as members of our family, intimate partner and our children, are particularly pertinent, although other significant relationships (e.g. colleagues, bosses, friends, teachers, therapists) will also allow us to see these hidden parts of us.

Relationship acts as a kind of boiling pot for our unconscious or negated parts, to arise and be seen. This gives us an opportunity to embody and include these aspects of our self, allowing us to grow, become whole and eventually utilise this energy.

In relationship, both positive and negative aspects of our self and the other are revealed. We will therefore feel both positive and negative emotions, in all relationships.

The "positive" emotions that arise are usually sought after and considered a sign of a good connection. I emphasise *usually* as some of us feel uncomfortable when we experience certain positive feelings in relationship. In this case we may be more familiar with the negative side, so our job is to find people who we feel safe with and who will allow us to become familiar with the positive aspects of relationship (e.g. safety, protectiveness, warmth, nourishment, companionship, fun, etc).

We will also of course experience "negative" emotions within relationships. We may think this indicates a problem with our self, the other person or the relationship itself. We may then engage in various habitual ways to try and fix the problem. Perhaps we try and change the other person, convince them our way is the right way, manipulate them, become demanding, blame them for their inadequacies, cut off or leave; so we feel okay again. Alternatively, we might adapt our self to fit in with what they want and need, concede to their wishes, blame ourselves, feel responsible for solving the problem and basically do anything so the relationship gets back to "normal"; so we feel okay again.

The one thing we don't usually do is realise, although this person or relationship triggered this "negative" emotion, it occurred within us. Thus it is an opportunity to embody an aspect of our self, which we haven't previously wanted to feel and see.

Taking responsibility for ALL our self is courageous and difficult work. We quite often have an idea about who we are and most likely want to feel and be seen in a certain way. Owning up to parts of us that aren't so "pretty" is therefore challenging.

Recognising the relationship has triggered a difficult emotion in us, is a good start. Owning this and taking responsibility for our emotional reaction is even better. Then we can acknowledge and include this part of us in our conscious self. Consequently, we are able to bring more consciousness into our relationships.[bb]

[bb] See box on the following page titled, "Emotional Energy in Relationship".

Emotional Energy in Relationship

Like a process of alchemy, the emotional boiling pot of relationship allows us an opportunity to transform; develop and grow. This opportunity will present itself many times in all our relationships. It is up to us however, to decide how we use it.

We may take responsibility for this emotional energy expressing itself inside of us, learning how to embody and harness it. Or we may avoid and deny this emotional expression, allowing the energy to unconsciously push and pull us.

Indeed, when two people's unconscious emotions arise in a relationship, one of two things usually occur. One or both people may recognise and harness their emotional energy, destroy the old and allow the creation of new life in the relationship. Here, they maintain responsibility for their emotions while bringing their concerns into the relationship. Alternatively, one or both people do not harness the emotional energy and continue to act out their habitual relational ways. The relationship then becomes stuck and stagnated in a familiar dance, or perhaps explodes into what seems like an unresolvable conflict.

Working in Relationship

While working through our psychological "stuff" with someone, it won't always be a smooth path. Through this relationship, as already alluded to, both our darkness and light is brought forth; so our experience will be one which feels both good and bad.

The good is that we will have a felt experience of what it means to be connected, supported and related to within a secure, "good enough" relationship. In the beginning this might feel unfamiliar and uncomfortable for some of us, so we might not be able to take in all the goodness initially. If however, we allow ourselves to gradually stay with and receive the care and support, we will notice how it nourishes, nurtures and warms us; a bit like drinking a hot chocolate by a warm fire on a cold winter's night.

There will also be times when this relationship triggers our long forgotten defences, wounds and hurts. Although this will probably feel like a bad thing at the time, it is actually positive. If in some part of us we can remember this is an opportune moment, to engage in our psychological work of becoming whole, we are then more likely to utilise these times to become more conscious.

If we are earnest about doing this work of being more whole, we may need (at some point) to decide whether we can do this work within current personal relationships, or whether for some parts we require a therapeutic relationship. Since relationships vary widely in their purpose and level of support, we may not be able to do all the work within particular relationships. There may be many reasons for this, but essentially, not all relationships will be conducive to certain aspects of our repair work.

To venture into the darkness of our emotional labyrinth, we

need to feel safe, supported and held. We also need to trust the other person has experience and understanding about the process we are required to undertake.

It is important to choose wisely; who we do this repair work with and who we don't do this work with. Once we have carefully chosen the person to do the work with, it is important we stay the course; even when "things" get tricky.

One thing is for certain, it will get tricky at times. It is uncomfortable to honestly face our self; the pain, the parts we don't want to see, our unconsciousness. So there will be times when we think we cannot or do not want to proceed on.

Ultimately it is our choice and responsibility to decide what we do at these crossroads. In making a decision however, it is generally best to bring our dilemma into the relationship.

Some of us though, might make a decision without the input of the other. Perhaps we think they will not be supportive, or that we know what we want so there is no need to talk about it. Maybe we secretly blame them, feel angry or don't want to reveal our vulnerability in this relationship. Here, we miss the opportunity of sharing our problem and perhaps getting the care, support or feedback we require.

Alternatively, we might not think about our own needs and just go along with the other. We may even "check in" with what they want and then make a decision based on this. Although we could bring our concern to the relationship, we probably defer to them and give more weight to their feelings then our own. Unconsciously we might believe they are responsible for our dilemma, so we approach them, secretly wanting them to fix it somehow. In this instance we miss the opportunity to be responsible for our self, be clear about our needs and be self-determining.

Finally, there might be a few of us who feel scared the other will retaliate or reject us, if we bring our concerns to them. So we don't approach them and remain stuck in our fear, unable to decide one way or the other. In this instance, we miss the opportunity of seeing, in reality, how they respond to us. Certainly, if we approach them and they do retaliate or reject us, then we probably need to decide whether we continue this type of relationship. There is also a possibility however, they will support us and assist us to get unstuck and continue our journey. But, if we don't take the risk of approaching the other, we will never know which response will actually occur, so we will continue to remain stuck and uncertain.

There is a balance to be had here. We bring our concerns into the relationship, while maintaining responsibility for our needs and the way we communicate them. Of course, our habitual ways of relating will often get in the way. So getting this balance is not going to be easy. Furthermore, even if we did get this balance, it doesn't mean the other person will always agree or give us what we need. Although ideally, we would work towards the needs of both people being met, the actual process of achieving this can be difficult to navigate, so we may often fall short of this ideal. It is in this *struggle* of relating however, that we learn more about our strengths and limitations, and thus understand what this *being human* is all about.

Wholeness can only be achieved through relationship.

Guide 3: Time

This psychological work of repair involves looking at ourselves deeply; facing the truth of where we have come from and who we are today. This process, literally, takes time.

There are No Quick Fixes!

When we truly understand this process of repair, we realise there is no "magic cure". This means, there is no weekend workshop or one-stop shop to quickly make everything better. We may attend a workshop to assist us on our path, but hoping this will *solve* everything is a bit like chasing rainbows. There is also no pill or potion that can do this work for us.[cc]

There is also no person who can "fix" and make everything better. We do need to do this work within a supportive relational context; this other person, however, isn't there to "cure" us. In this work of repair, they are here to gently allow us to bring forth all that has been negated, kept unconscious and inhibited our aliveness. This provides us with an opportunity to embrace our full human beingness.

Since our modern world is largely based on immediacy and quick fixes, we sometimes bring this expectation to our psychological work. We might imagine this repair work to be a bit like fixing a machine or computer. Perhaps we expect it to be done in the time we have grown accustomed to with the speed of technology in our modern world. Both these expectations are false. We are a complex organic system, more aligned with the nature of a plant or tree than a machine, computer or any sort of technological instrument.

[cc] Medication cannot do this psychological work for us. I think it is important to acknowledge though that some people may require medication, for a certain period, alongside this work of psychological growth. Furthermore, for those people who, for various reasons, cannot go through and do all the required psychological work, medication may support them to gain some stability and quality of life, which may not be possible without it. On the other hand, it is also important to acknowledge, our social and health systems are not necessarily conducive or supportive of people engaging in the depth of psychological work they may require, and so medication often becomes their only option.

We Need "Time" to Grow

A plant requires time to grow. If we *force* it to grow faster (e.g. by straining it), we interfere with its natural direction and may even dislodge it from the soil. This is the same with our psychological growth.

Patience, and a willingness to take each step along our individual path of repair is essential. Given this, we may at times become frustrated with our process, thinking we "should" be progressing faster. We might begin to doubt ourselves and wonder if we are doing something wrong. Maybe we become angry with the person who is assisting us. Perhaps we become disillusioned and feel like giving-up. At these times, it is good to bring our doubt, frustration and despair into the relationship. Since this path is not a straight or linear journey, it is also okay to get a second opinion, further guidance or take a rest. We can also gently remind ourselves, this work of repair and becoming whole will take time.

Repair in service of our wholeness is a life-long journey.

In Summary

In understanding how a house is built from the ground up, we know what conditions are necessary for this house to stand tall and secure, even when a storm comes. We also understand how to repair and restore parts of this house, which haven't been built so well or are in need of a little extra care. This is the same with us. When we understand the conditions necessary for us to grow into whole human beings, we will know how to repair, restore or give a little extra care to those parts of us which are not secure.

This book has focused on the importance of our earliest childhood as the basis of our psychological development. The conditions which occur in these earliest years (from utero to seven years of age) have a significant impact on who we experience ourselves to be, and how we see and interact with the world. The majority of us (50%-70%) have experienced "good enough" conditions in these early years of childhood.

For the remainder of us, whose relational environment was not so favourable, we were unable to grow-up simply being who we are. We were required to adapt our self, so we could survive in a relational environment unable to embrace our wholeness. Consequently, we were unable to move through early developmental phases with our whole being and aliveness intact, but needed to negate some parts. These parts remained in our unconscious and thus did not have the opportunity to grow and develop along with the rest of our self. Fortunately, we have the possibility throughout our lifetime to claim, make conscious and integrate these forgotten parts of our wholeness. This means, until we take our last breath, we still have the opportunity to grow into a psychologically mature and whole person.

In some ways, we have all had to adapt ourselves. We have all learnt, to more or less degrees, to be a certain way; to fit into a family system, community, culture and the world. I am not suggesting this is always negative, as we are essentially inter-dependent, and grow through being in community with others. Perhaps though, we may benefit by maintaining a curiosity about these familial, cultural and societal structures we emerge within. And like a child playfully asking "why", question how these structures have *helped* and *hindered* our becoming fully human.

I want to finish by stating that in writing this book, my intention is to encourage a deep look at whether our relational experiences, particularly in our early years, were conducive to becoming whole human beings. To be clear, I am not promoting a sense of blame towards our mothers, fathers, other significant relationships or institutions in society. I am encouraging an *active* exploration of what it means to be fully human. So that we may *all* live in a way which is conducive to our (and others) full humanity. Considering our earliest relationships lay the foundation for this and we grow within a social milieu, it is prudent to examine these. Did we feel safe? (Do we feel safe now?) Could we get our needs met? (Can we get our needs met now?) Were we free to be who we really are? (Are we free now to be who we really are?) Were we valued for just being? (Are we valued now for just being?) In this way we can see the factors which were (and are currently) "good enough" for our growth as human beings, and the factors which were (and are currently) "not good enough".

In this process of looking deeply, we will have many feelings (positive and negative) about our mothers, fathers, significant others and various societal institutions (e.g. those related to; education, religion, justice, healthcare, politics). These feelings need to be felt and worked through. We cannot skip steps in this process.

For example, we might try to prematurely forgive and thereby not acknowledge our real anger. Alternatively, we might hastily cut contact to avoid working through our pain and grief. We need to acknowledge, be with and feel through the anger, fear, grief, betrayal, frustration, sadness, shock, disbelief, gratitude, joy and aliveness. By courageously embracing our experience and creatively making use of it, we actively engage in the process of repair and becoming fully human.

If we do the work, as suggested in this book, we have the opportunity to grow into our wholeness. Gradually, we may feel less and less at the mercy of unconscious conflict, both within us and in our relationships.[93] Our sense of self may become more authentic, cohesive, resilient and able to tolerate a greater emotional range.[94] We may also grow in our capacity for engaging in fulfilling and constructive relationships; in our personal lives and in the communities we live.[95]

Over time we may begin to appreciate the impact our relational experiences have had on us, including our resultant strengths and limitations. Having authentically grieved our loss, including understanding there is no going back to get what we missed, we can begin to live our future with the growth, maturity and security we have earned. Although life will not suddenly become easy and problem free, we now have the inner resources and strength to deal with the storms which will inevitably arise; allowing us to creatively engage in the unfolding of this human journey.

It is my hope that in reading this book, some of the mystery of growing into a psychologically whole person has been dispelled. And that rather than running around trying to feel better through means which are not beneficial, we will be encouraged to *honestly* do the psychological work.

Even if the beginning of our life was not conducive to us growing up with our whole self intact, there is a path of repair. The essential nature of our "being and aliveness" is fluid, organic, creative, alive and whole. So we all have the seeds of this wholeness within us. It is now up to us however, to discover the nourishment for this seed to grow. So may each of us seek and receive the support we require for this journey, for we cannot do this alone.

If we want to repair our house (or wholeness of self), we will need to do the work and put in the effort. This is essential, for without it, our hope is empty and will eventually result in hopelessness. Hope needs to be backed up with effort and skilful ways. Just like a builder will not sit on a log, looking at a house, hoping the repairs and renovations will get done. We too cannot sit and stare at life as it passes us by, hoping that something will change, without actually doing something about it. If we do not look deeply, check what needs to be repaired, get the assistance we require and do the dirty work, we will never reap the benefits. There is hope, no matter how difficult our journey has been thus far. But hope without skilful means, is simply a dream unrealised.

And finally, in doing this work of repair to become whole human beings, we do not erase our history or wounds. Neither do we become whole in spite of our history and woundedness. We become whole, *because* of our history and woundedness.

JUST AS EACH THREAD IS ESSENTIAL IN THE COMPLETED

GARMENT, SO EVERY SINGLE ONE OF US, WHILE BEING

ONE OF MANY, IS VITALLY IMPORTANT TO THE FABRIC OF

THIS WORLD. SO AS WE CONTINUE TO TAKE THE STEPS ON

OUR RESPECTIVE PATHS, LET US HOLD EACH OTHER IN

HEART AND MIND, KNOWING WE ARE NOT ALONE

ON THIS JOURNEY.

~ ♥ ~

Appendix

This appendix contains a brief description of Attachment Theory and Separation-Individuation Theory.[dd]

Attachment Theory

The psychological science of attachment, which originally described the emotional bond between a baby and mother, is an ever-expanding area.[ee] Rooted in a long history of psychoanalysis, analyst David Levy was perhaps the first person in 1937 to bring attention to the importance of this relationship. Ten years later, Rene Spritz ignited much debate about whether the classical Freudian idea of being driven by our instinctual desires, for food and sex, left a gap in our understanding of what it means to be human. It was also around this time that people such as Melanie Klein, Ronald Fairbairn, Michael Balint, Donald Winnicott and later Harry Guntrip formed what is now known as the British Object Relations Theorists; where the developing infant and child is understood to need another person (or "object", as called in this theory) to attach to, internalise and grow from. In America, people such as Karen Horney and Erich Fromme were also developing ideas and theories related to the interpersonal realm. These thinkers pioneered the idea that people are motivated by more than

---

[dd] Even though I describe the theories in their originality, with the mother as the primary caregiver, I would like to make room for the possibility of other people also being primary caregiver's (e.g. father, extended family member or other support person).

[ee] The ensuing information about the history of attachment is taken from, Karen, R. (1994). *Becoming Attached: First Relationships and how they Shape our Capacity to Love.* NY: Oxford University Press. This book provides a more detailed history and extensive coverage of attachment theory.

instinctual drives, and that they have a primary need to connect and have meaningful relationships.

The person however, we think foremost of in regard to Attachment Theory is John Bowlby. Most likely influenced by the Object Relations Theorists mentioned above, he went on in the 1940's to fan the debate about the importance of mother-love and the detrimental effects of maternal deprivation. Bowlby's research continued for many years in the United Kingdom, coinciding with Harry Harlow's experiments in America in the late 1950's, which showed the negative impact of a lack of attachment and love on rhesus monkeys.

Although the evidence for the importance of mother-love was growing, the field of psychology at the time was dominated by behaviourists views (e.g. Ivan Pavlov and James Watson), where the word "love" was somewhat frowned upon as it was considered unscientific. In the psychoanalytic wings of psychology, some Freudians also had difficulty adjusting to the idea that the time in a child's life before the pre-school years could be central to development.

Around this time, Mary Ainsworth also began studying infant behaviour. She was particularly interested in understanding the harm she witnessed when babies and young children were separated from their mothers. This was around the Second World War in England, when many children were put in orphanages. Ainsworth wanted to know whether it was the separation per-say that was harmful, or if it was the maternal deprivation accompanying the separation that was the cause of harm. She was instrumental in clarifying this aspect of Bowlby's theory, stating the harm included three dimensions, namely; insufficient care, neglect or maltreatment and separations from the mother. In the 1960's she went on to develop an assessment of parenting style through a research paradigm known as "The Strange Situation". Through this research, with infants and their mother's, she postulated three categories of attachment.

The three attachment styles Ainsworth identified include; secure, insecure-ambivalent and insecure-avoidant. Babies categorised with a **secure** attachment, sought their mother when distressed and were confident of her availability. They were upset when she left the room in The Strange Situation and eagerly greeted her when she returned, allowing her to hug and comfort them until they were soothed.[96] **Insecure-ambivalent** attached babies on the other hand, tended to be overtly anxious and clingy as well as demanding. In The Strange Situation they were distressed when their mother left, but upon her return even though they went to her, arched away angrily or went limp and were unable to be soothed.[97] The **insecure-avoidant** attached babies seemed to depend less on their mother as a secure base, although they could be demanding and angry. In The Strange Situation they could show just as much distress when their mother left as other babies, albeit in a more covert way, however upon her return they did not show interest in her.[98]

Many years later in 1986, one of Ainsworth's students, namely Mary Main, upon re-studying the data in The Strange Situation paradigm, identified a forth category of attachment called **disorganised/disoriented**.[99] The babies in this category showed unusual or no set pattern in their response to their mother leaving and returning in The Strange Situation. They perhaps sat in the corner silently, rocked or banged their heads against the wall when she left. Upon her return some of the infants started to move towards their mother, but then froze or flapped their arms in fear. Others approached their mother, but with their back to her or in a sideways-step motion. These infants were seen to exhibit an approach-avoidance sort of style. Compared to the secure and insecure types, they did not seem to have an organised attachment pattern or system.

Separation-Individuation Theory

Around the same time attachment theory originated, Hungarian born psychiatrist Margaret Mahler and her team formulated a theory of "normal" child development.[ff] This was based upon observations of infants and toddlers interacting with caregivers, strangers and other children. In this theory, "separation" refers to the child's growing understanding they are separate from their mother and that reality has limitations. While "individuation", refers to the development of a sense of self or identity.

After the first few weeks of infancy (originally termed the normal autistic phase), Mahler suggested babies progress to what she called the normal symbiotic phase (4-6 weeks until 5 months of age). At this phase, although aware of their mother, the infant feels as if their mother and they are in union. From here (5 months onward), the infant goes through an extended separation-individuation phase, where they slowly begin to differentiate themselves from their mother ("me" from "not me") and develop a separate sense of self.

The first part of this separation-individuation phase, Mahler called **hatching** (5 to 9 months). The infant here starts to be more conscious of their differentiation, becomes aware of their wider environment and uses their mother to orientate themselves in their expanded world. For example, the infant's eyes will move away

---

[ff] See, Mahler, M. S., Pine, F., Bergman, A. (2008). *The Psychological Birth of the Human Infant: Symbiosis and Individuation.* UK: Hatchette.

from the mother but then check back to her. The second part of this phase is called **practicing** (9 to 16 months). Here the infant moves about on their own, crawling, standing up and walking. They also begin to explore more actively and feel overjoyed (i.e. grandiose and omnipotent) by their abilities. They will move away from their mother, but not go too far and will check back to see if she is there. Although they are becoming more independent, the infant here still does not experience itself as separate from their mother. The mother's ability to be available and stay attuned, while conveying expectation and confidence in their child, lays the foundation for the child to successfully navigate the remainder of the separation-individuation phase.[100]

The third part of this phase (15 months and beyond) is called **rapproachment**. Because of greater mobility and increasing communication, the toddler here experiences increased autonomy, self-reliance and ability to say "No". This sense of self-determination is juxtaposed by feelings of frustration, as their experiences, emotions and desires conflict with the limitations of reality. This is also the time when the toddler starts to understand they are separate from their mother. This realisation of separateness results in ambivalent feelings; on the one hand excitement and power, while on the other anxiety and fear.[101] The developing child requires a responsive other to navigate this ambivalence. This includes, celebrating their strengths, while holding their vulnerabilities, as well as attuning to sudden shifts of dependence and independence.

The fourth part of this phase is called **on the way to object constancy**, which Mahler suggested continues throughout life. "Object" refers to relationship with a person, and specifically with the mother in this theory. A mostly good loving image is internalised, providing the child with a sense of safety, security and comfort, just as the actual mother had.[102] When the parenting is "good enough", the child can hold both good and bad aspects of mother in mind at the same time, and feel generally satisfied or comforted. Furthermore, as the mother has become internalised, the child does not require her constant presence. So when the child or mother goes away, the child is okay as they know the relationship will still be there when they come back.

Embedded in this fourth phase is the idea of **self-constancy**, where the child begins to stand as a separate and unique person. They begin to know themselves as someone with strengths and weaknesses, who is basically okay. Over time their sense of self becomes more stable and continuous, so they do not feel or act radically differently from one situation to the next. This stability allows the child to grow feeling okay about themselves, with a good self-esteem and sense of confidence.

Acknowledgments

Thank you to Gloria Ward and Sharman for your proof reading and suggestions in the editing process. Your encouragement and constructive criticisms were a blessing to the crafting of this written work.

Thank you to all my family and friends who have kept interested in my writing, over the last ten years. You have held me to the task of finishing and getting this one out into the world; I appreciate that. I am also grateful to all the people who said, "Hey when's it finished, I want to read it." Being reminded about the possible benefit this book may have for others, inspired me to continue writing in moments of self-doubt.

Finally, a special thank you to my psychotherapist for the last five and half years. Because of the dedication you have to your craft and the therapeutic work I was able to do with you; this book was able to come into existence. I am sincerely grateful.

Reference Notes

Part I

[1] Schore, 2012
[2] Schore, 2012
[3] Kalef, 2014
[4] Antunovic, 2015 (2nd citation)
[5] Antunovic, 2015
[6] Schore, 2012
[7] Gerhardt, 2015
[8] Schore, 2012
[9] Heller, 1997
[10] Schore, 2012
[11] Blom & Bergman, 2013
[12] Newton, 2008
[13] Newton, 2008
[14] Newton, 2008
[15] Newton, 2008
[16] Newton, 2008
[17] Newton, 2008
[18] Newton, 2008
[19] Wallin, 2007
[20] Schore, 2012
[21] Symington, 2002
[22] Guntrip, 1968; Laing, 1965
[23] Guntrip, 1968; Symington, 2002
[24] Symington, 2007
[25] Maroda, 2010
[26] Symington, Symington, Symington & Symington, 2003
[27] Schore, 2012
[28] Schore, 2012
[29] Schore, 2012
[30] Schore, 2012
[31] Schore, 2012
[32] Schore, 2012
[33] Guntrip, 1968
[34] Winnicott, 1960
[35] Fisher, 2017

[36] Siegal, 2008
[37] Winnicott, 1996; Wallin, 2007
[38] Gerhardt, 2015
[39] Pinker, 2014
[40] Schore, 2012
[41] Schore, 2012

PART II
Phase One
[42] Schore, 2012
[43] Gerhardt, 2015
[44] Gerhardt, 2015
[45] Gerhardt, 2015
[46] Wallin, 2007
[47] Laing, 1965
[48] Guntrip, 1968
[49] Johnson, 1994
[50] Johnson, 1994
[51] Johnson, 1994
[52] Guntrip, 1968
[53] Wallin, 2007
[54] Jakobi
[55] McWilliams, 2006
[56] McWilliams, 1994
[57] Orloff, 2017
Phase Two
[58] Newton, 2008
[59] Kalef, 2014
[60] Wallin, 2007
[61] Newton, 2008; Gerhardt, 2015
[62] Schore, 2012; Kolk, 2014
[63] Newton, 2008
[64] Gerhardt, 2015
[65] Johnson, 1994
Phase Three
[66] Wallin, 2007
[67] Blum, 2001
[68] Blum, 2001
[69] Blum, 2001
[70] Blum, 2001

[71] Wallin, 2007
[72] Fisher, 2017
[73] Johnson, 1994
[74] Horney, 1991; Horney,1992
[75] Horney, 1991; Horney, 1992
[76] Buber, 2010
[77] Buber, 2010
[78] Buber, 2010
[79] Johnson, 1987
[80] Wallin, 2007

Phase Four
[81] Blum, 2001
[82] Blum, 2001
[83] Blum, 2001
[84] Blom & Bergman, 2013
[85] Boyd, n.d.
[86] Winnicott, 1971
[87] Schore, 2012
[88] Schore, 2012
[89] Schore, 2012
[90] Spinelli, 1997
[91] Symington, 2002

PART III
[92] Winnicott, 1971
[93] Winnicott, 1996
[94] McWilliams, 2004
[95] McWilliams, 2004; Winnicott, 1996

Appendix
[96] Karen, 1994
[97] Karen, 1994
[98] Karen, 1994
[99] Wallin, 2007
[100] Blom & Bergman, 2013
[101] Blom & Bergman, 2013
[102] Blom &Bergman, 2013

Bibliography

Antunovic, E. (2015). *The Second Nine Months: Exterogestation and the Need to be Held.* Retrieved from BOBA: www.boba.com

Bauer, J. (2002). *The Myth of the First Three Years: A New Understanding of Early Brain Development and Lifelong Learning.* New York: Free Press.

Blom, I., & Bergman, A. (2013). Observing Development: A Comparative View of Attachment Theory and Separation-Individuation Theory. In J. E. Bettmann, D. D. Friedman, & (Eds.), *Attachment-Based Clinical Work with Children and Adolescents (Essential Clinical Work Series)* (pp. 9-43). NY: Springer.

Blum, H. P. (2001). *Separation-Individuation Theory and Attachment Theory*. Retrieved from APA Sagepub; Pennsylvania State University: www.apa.sagepub.com

Boyd, R. (n.d.). *The Perfectionist / Obsessional (Rigid).* Retrieved June 23, 2018, from Energetics Institute: http://energeticsinstitute.com.au/psychotherapy-counselling/characterology/perfectionist-obsessional-rigid/

Buber, M. (2010). *I and Thou*. USA: Martino Publishing.

Campbell, J. (1949). *The Hero with a Thousand Faces*. United States: Pantheon Books.

Fisher, J. (2017). *Healing the Fragmented Selves of Trauma Survivors: Overcoming Internal Self-Alienation.* NY: Routledge.

Gerhardt, S. (2015). *Why Love Matters: How affection shapes the baby's brain.* London, UK: Routledge.

Granju, K., & Sears, W. (1999). *Attachment Parenting: Instinctive Care for Your Baby and Young Child.* Atria.

Guntrip, H. (1968). *Schizoid Phenomena, Object Relations and the Self.* London: Karnac Books.

Heller, S. (1997). *The Vital Touch: How Intimate Contact with Your baby Leads To Happier, Healthier Development*.

Holt Paperbacks.

Herman, J. L. (1994). *Trauma and Recovery: From Domestic Abuse to Political Terror.* London: Pandora.

Horney, K. (1991). *Neurosis and Human Growth: The Struggle Towards Self-Realization.* NY, London: W.W. Norton & Co.

Horney, K. (1992). *Our Inner Conflicts: A Constructive Theory of Neurosis.* NY, London: W.W. Norton & Company.

Jakobi, L. (n.d.). *The Schizoid Personality: An Ego That Has Not Properly Begun to Be.* Retrieved from Integral Healing Centre: www.integralhealingcentre.com

Johnson, S. M. (1987). *Humanizing the Narcissistic Style.* NY, London: W.W. Norton & Company.

Johnson, S. M. (1994). *Character Styles: .* NY, London: W.W. Norton & Company.

Kalef, M. (2014). *The Secret life of Babies: How Our Prebirth and Birth Experiences Shape Our World.* North Atlantic Books.

Karen, R. (1994). *Becoming Attached: First Relationships and how they Shape our Capacity to Love.* NY: Oxford University Press.

Klein, M. (1997). *Envy and Gratitude and other works, 1946-1963.* Random House.

Laing, R. (1965). *The Divided Self:An Existential Study in Sanity and Madness.* Harmondsworth: Penguin.

Levine, A., & Heller, R. (2012). *Attached: The New Science of Adult Attachment and How it Can Help You Find and Keep Love.* USA: Penguin Putnam Inc.

Mahler, M. S., Pine, F., & Bergman, A. (2008). *The Psychological Birth of the Human Infant: Symbiosis and Individuation.* UK: Hatchette.

Maroda, K. J. (2010). *Psychodynamic Technique: Working with Emotion in the Therapeutic Relationship.* NY: The Guildford Press.

McWilliams, N. (1994). *Psychoanalytic Diagnosis: Understanding Personality Structure in the Clinical Process.* NY, London: The Guilldford Press.

McWilliams, N. (1999). *Psychoanalytic Case Formulation.* New York; London: Guildford Press.

McWilliams, N. (2004). *Psychoanalytic Psychotherapy: A Practitioner's Guide.* NY, London: The Guildford Press.

McWilliams, N. (2006). Some Thoughts about Schizoid Dynamics. *The Psychoanalytic Review*, 93(1):1-24.

Newton, R. P. (2008). *The Attachment Connection: Parenting a Secure amd Confident Child Using the Science of Attachment Theory.* New Harbinger Publications.

Orloff, J. (2017). *The Empath's Survival Guide: Life Strategies for Sensitive People (Audio).* Sounds True.

Pinker, S. (2014). *The Village Effect: Why Face-to-Face Contact Matters.* London : Atlantic Books.

Rinpoche, T. (2013). *The Five Buddha Families and The Eight Consciousnesses.* Retrieved from Rinpoche.com: www.rinpoche.com

Rothschild, B. (2000). *The Body Remembers: The Psychophysiology of Trauma and Trauma Treatment.* NY, London: W.W. Norton & Company.

Safran, J. D., & Muran, J. C. (2000). *Negotiating the Therapuetic Alliance.* NY, London: The Guildford Press.

Shore, A. N. (2012). *The Science of the Art of Psychotherapy.* NY: W.W Norton & Company.

Siegel, D. J. (2008). *Neurobiology of "We" (CD-Audio).* Louisville, CO, US: Sounds True Inc.

Spinelli, E. (1994). *Demystifying Therapy.* London: Constable.

Spinelli, E. (1997). *Tales of Un-Knowing: Therapuetic Encounters from an Existential Perspective.* London: Gerald Duckworth & Co.Ltd.

Symington, N. (2002). *A Pattern of Madness.* London: Karnac.

Symington, N. (2007). *Becoming a Person through Psychoanalysis.* London; New York: Karnac.

Symington, N., Symington, J., Symington, A., & Symington, D. (2003). *How to Choose a Therapist.* London; New York: Karnac.

Van der Kolk, B. (2014). *The Body Keeps the Score: Mind, Brain and Body in a Transformation of Trauma.* UK: Penguin.

Wallin, D. J. (2007). *Attachment in Psychotherapy.* NY: The Guildford Press.

Weiss, H., Johanson, G., Monda, L., & (Eds.). (2015). *Hakomi Mindfulness-Centred Somatic Psychotherapy: A Comprehensive Guide to Theory and Practice.* NY, London: W.W. Norton & Company.

Wilber, K. (2016). *Integral Meditation: Mindfulness as a Path to Grow Up, Wake Up and Show Up in Your Life.* Boulder, Colorado: Shambala Publications Inc.

Winnicott, D. W. (1960). Ego Distortion in Terms of True and False Self. In D. W. Winnicott, *The Maturational Processes and the Facilitating Environment: Studies in the Theory of Emotional Development* (pp. 140-152). London: Karnac.

Winnicott, D. W. (1971). *Playing and Reality.* London, NY: Routledge.

Winnicott, D. W. (1996). *Thinking About Children.* USA: A Merloyd Lawrence Book.

Winnicott, D. W. (2011). *Reading Winnicott.* East Sussex: Routledge.